A Broken Heart Still Beats

A Broken Heart Still Beats
A grieving mother's journey toward peace

By
Nancy Carswell

Copyright 2024 – All rights reserved.

The content contained within this book may not be reproduced, duplicated, or transmitted without direct written permission from the author or the publisher.

Under no circumstances will any blame or legal responsibility be held against the publisher, or author, for any damages, reparation, or monetary loss due to the information contained within this book, either directly or indirectly.

Legal Notice:

This book is copyright protected. It is only for personal use. You may not amend, distribute, sell, use, quote or paraphrase any content within this book without the consent of the author or the publisher.

Disclaimer Notice:

The information herein is for educational and entertainment purposes only. Readers acknowledge that the author is not engaged in the rendering of legal, financial, medical, or professional advice. The content within this book is based on the author's real-life experiences. Please consult a licensed professional before attempting any techniques outlined in this book. By reading this document, the reader agrees that under no circumstances is the author responsible for any losses, direct or indirect, that are incurred because of the use of the information contained in this document, including but not limited to errors, omissions, or inaccuracies.

Table of Contents

1. Grief Description
2. A Little of the Back Story
3. The Diagnosis
4. That Horrible Phone Call
5. By His Side
6. Loving Support
7. Taking Control (of letting go)
8. Hospice
9. Colton's Decision
10. A Promise Kept
11. Obituary /Celebration of Life
12. My Rock
13. Grief Settles In
14. Dreams
15. Grief, and Gratitude?
16. Back to Work
17. A Leap of Faith
18. A Promotion and a Pandemic
19. Journey to the Island
20. Self-care
21. The Blog
22. Learning to Live with Grief
23. Something New

Prologue

Grief is universal. It affects every aspect of our lives, changing the way we think, the way we look and feel, even our entire belief system. It can stop us in our tracks. It can unite or divide us.

The absolute worst thing that I could have ever imagined has happened to me. It is the loneliest feeling. Still, I know I am not alone. If you found this today, know that I am here struggling like you, with this heavy, unkind, and unfair emotional response...grief. It will change you in ways you have never imagined. It takes you to a place that is so dark, you will wonder if you ever see light again. Your identity and purpose have been stripped away, and you must start from scratch to find your path to peace. This is where my journey began.

For Colton

Chapter 1

Grief Description

They said I should have started writing right away. They said it would have been therapeutic. But honestly, who are 'they' anyways? I could barely keep my thoughts straight or string more than a few words together. I remember that shortly after Colton died, I could barely remember anything, and that was horrifying to me. There were so many details that I was struggling to hold on to, but it felt like my brain was broken. I knew my son better than anyone on earth, yet the fog was so thick I felt stuck in it. Then eventually, an endless commentary began in my head. Things I had wanted to say but did not get the chance. All day in the background and all night while desperate to fall asleep. Somehow, when a memory struck me, I eventually began to write things down as they came flooding in. Now, years later, I realize that the story has no end. You have a similar one, a story of loss.

So much has been written about grief. The classic stages, as follows: denial, anger, bargaining, depression, and acceptance. I am sure that this is how it goes. However, I do not believe that these stages are true for child loss in particular, at least in my case. There are simply no rules that apply to the utter devastation that this causes. For me, the stages are all at once, backwards, or forwards, depending on the day.

There are no fixed rules as to how you will deal with grief. Wouldn't it be handy if it were the same for everyone? If we could simply work through the steps and stages of grief and then that is it, you are done!? Oh, if it were just that easy! Here are my thoughts on grief:

I believe that what a grieving mother thinks about grief and what the rest of humanity thinks are different in so many ways. First, it depends on the grief we are discussing. For example, if your pet dies, yes, it is incredibly sad, and you will mourn the loss for a time and may or may not get another pet to share your life with. It may take time, but you may find there is room for another pet in your heart and in your home. Your lost pet becomes a favorite memory. When Colton died, and I was back at work, I had someone say to me, "I know it is hard. I had to put my dog down last week because he had Cancer too." Um, sorry, NOT the same thing and no, you do NOT know how hard it is. I still shake my head and wonder how someone could have been so callous and/or uneducated as to have said that to me so early in my grief experience!

If a friend dies, it can fill your heart with sorrow and flood you with memories of the connection you had with them. You will continue to dwell on your loss for a long time. But eventually, the pain eases and you remember all the wonderful memories of the good times you shared and can move forward and accept the loss as a beautiful chapter in your life. When you think of them, the dominant feeling is the love that you had for them.

When it became evident that my parents were nearing the end of their life journey, it was a sorrowful experience. Your mind and thoughts are filled with all the time spent with them, the good and the bad over the years. You are filled with grief and uncertainty of what your life would be like without them in it. It is the natural order of things to eventually lose your parents. As adults, we gradually watch their physical and mental decline and along the way become accustomed to the fact that they will leave us. We have time to prepare our hearts for the burden. In the best-case scenario, we can be there when they pass and witness the end of their life's journey. This was the case with my father. Colton and I were able to be there with two of my three siblings for his passing and it was with both sorrow and awe that we watched him go.

However, there is grief unlike any other, when it is unnatural and out of the order of things. When there is no way to prepare your heart and mind for it. When the sheer power and force of it is beyond measure. The loss of your child. The Stages of Grief mean absolutely nothing to you. Your body is in a state of utter shock. You are unable to catch your breath because there is a crushing weight on your chest. Your eyes are swollen shut and the blood vessels surrounding them have exploded and you look like you have been punched in the face because you have cried and will continue to cry oceans of tears. Your joints and muscles ache like you have been slammed into a concrete wall. You are beyond tired but cannot sleep because every time you close your eyes you see your dead child and know that from this moment on your future is just a vast chasm of time that you will spend without him. Inside of you there is a scream like no other, and it just lives there now. For as much as you scream, as much as you cry, yell, swear, sob, pound your pillow or the floors or the walls, for as much as you throw things or just sit in silence unable to move, the strength of that scream is simply unable to get out. It is now the state in which you exist. Over time it may retreat into the backstage left of your mind, dormant, only to rush to the front and center of the stage needing to be seen at the most inopportune times. You may be able to harness this for a time, but eventually the sheer weight of it begs you to let go...

I know that grieving parents around the world are feeling this. Yet, there are days when I feel like it is just me. Sometimes grief puts you in solitary confinement.

I had the incredible privilege of being Colton's mom for 26 years, 2 months, and 4 days, until Cancer made him say goodbye.

In the early days of my loss, I joined a couple of online groups of mothers who had lost their sons. They are closed groups for a reason: no one wants to hear what is really going on inside of us, because they know there is nothing they can do. And we cannot even properly speak to those brave souls who attempt to console us in the beginning, because sometimes no words come out even though there are millions of words lined up in a queue, waiting. And sometimes, there is not a single word to be found.

It was so difficult to read all these mothers' stories and how they were feeling. Many wanted to end their life and join their sons. Many others chose drug therapy, listing the cocktails of meds prescribed by their doctors, as well as the side effects that they were experiencing. Others just drank themselves to sleep, turned to food for comfort, and described their struggles with their spouses who were grieving differently. So many, like me, experienced a vast array of health issues related to shock and PTSD of watching their child die, such as bleeding ulcers, hair loss, muscle pain, and insomnia.

People see us carrying on. They see us working, looking after others, taking care of the house, the cooking, and the chores, all of it. So, we must have moved on. So, we must be 'over it.' So, we must be ok, right?

We will never ever be who we were before. We have no choice but to do what we do to survive, and the fact that we change as a result is inevitable. 'Ok' is a relative term. After a time, I withdrew from the groups. They gave me a sense of community, yes, but I found them overwhelmingly negative. Now, don't get me wrong, I was not the positive one in the group, there was not a single Suzie Sunshine in the house. I had to opt out because it was making my own grief worse to be inundated with these posts all day while I was struggling to get out of bed and take a shower. It was just too much. When I find a group that speaks to me now, I follow if I find it beneficial. If it offers me more insight or if I find it upbuilding and motivational. Although these groups showed me that I was not alone, and I was free to express whatever I wanted about my grief without judgement, it was not these dark, sorrowful groups that were the therapy, support, or information that I was searching for.

I was on autopilot. I felt like I was outside of myself. I am completely aware of how this sounds. However, if you are grieving, this is how it is. I saw that I was going through the motions of being alive, even functioning quite well at times, but in my mind.... oh, no. Nope.

I needed to sit with my grief. I needed to breathe. Why did it seem that I was unable to do either?

Eventually, through lots of online searches, information about the mind, healing, and meditation would begin to resonate with me. I will be the first one to admit that my brain is creating thoughts at top speed, on overdrive, all day, and all night sometimes as well. Even now, I am reminded to "shut your brain off!" by my loving husband, because I am constantly talking about plans, new projects, my latest ideas, blah blah blah. I get it. My mind is too busy. It is my coping mechanism. One of many that help me through my days now. It is like if I can keep my mind busy thinking of things to do, then I will somehow magically not cry today, or feel hopeless today, or feel broken today. Of course, this is complete crap and has never worked for me, but I somehow continue to do it anyway. So, finding ways to sit, just sit and clear all that clutter of thought and emotion, has really helped in finding my path to peace.

There are many aspects of grief, and each piece of it feels like a slap in the face, as I soon learned.

What do I mean by finding my path to peace? Is this even an achievable goal, considering what I had gone through?

Am I referring to sitting under a tree somewhere singing Kumbaya? No, unless that is your thing, then you do you. For me, it simply means a calm state of acceptance and finding a measure of joy and passion for life that will accompany the rest of my days. A lofty goal indeed! It was obvious. I did not know grief yet; it was just the beginning. I have had, and still have, a long journey ahead of me. A perilous, exhausting, uphill climb through the mud, the blood, and the heartache of loss. You can try to find your own shortcut, good for you if you do, but I think you will find that you will have to climb this ladder rung by rung...

Chapter 2

A little of the Back Story

Looking back, Colton went through many challenges with his health. As a toddler and in his early school years, he suffered from chronic ear/nose/throat issues that came with extremely high fever. I was forever taking him to the Doctor's office, then specialists, and quite often the Emergency room. These constant infections led to a lack of the ability to concentrate at school, and I spent countless hours with workbooks at home, teaching him the basics one-on-one which I found he could grasp quite easily. A group of teachers, speech pathologists, and learning assistants told me that he would always need extra help in school due to his learning disability. I told them, quite angrily, that he did not have a learning disability, he had health issues. So, we agreed to disagree. By middle school, Colton made the Work Habits honor roll, and by high school he was on the Academic Honor Roll. Then his health started to take a turn for the worse.

During his Grad year he suffered from a condition called Pilonidal Sinus. It usually starts as an infection in a hair follicle and creates pockets of infection that require surgery. In Colton's case it required 2 surgeries, lots of antibiotics, hospital time and in-home care, the process taking the better part of a year. All the while, working hard to complete a trades program to become a welder.

Then, leading up to and including his 19th birthday, he suffered an extreme sinus infection that moved in behind his left eye, moving his eye over with the swelling. The infection spread so quickly, causing extreme headaches that took us back to the Emergency room on several occasions. These were simply misdiagnosed as migraines and treated as such. Thankfully, our family Doctor happened to be there one night, saw Colton, and said, "that's no migraine, he needs surgery immediately." They went in at the corner of his eye as well as his nose to drain the infection which if left untreated, may have burst, killing him. It was a narrow escape.

By late 2014, Colton had told me about a spot that the dental hygienist had seen at the back of his tongue during a routine cleaning. Colton never missed a dental appointment and had never had a single cavity. He then tried to open his mouth and show me this spot, but I could not really see much. It was a small white dot. He said it did not hurt but that the dentist would keep an eye on it. Eventually they scraped it, and the test came back fine, and we did not worry about it. Over time, several months to a year, he mentioned that it was starting to be painful when he ate, like a canker sore. By this time, my husband Randy and I had been transferred from Prince George B.C. to Edmonton Alberta for work, 8 hours away. He had to make all his own Doctor appointments and follow through by himself. He was living on his own with his girlfriend and they were living life. All grown up.

Chapter 3

The diagnosis

The following Thanksgiving, 2016, Randy had taken a week to go back to Prince George to go hunting with his eldest son Bailey and his father, a 3-generation trip. Colton and his girlfriend decided to take a road trip and visit me. We had such a wonderful time that weekend, just the 3 of us. It remains one of my fondest memories. October in Edmonton is cold! We wore our winter coats to take Louie our Frenchton pup for walks in the nearby park. I took a video on my phone of them playing on the merry go round like a couple of little kids, then going down the slide taking the puppy with them. We just enjoyed our time together immensely, going to the West Edmonton Mall where we played mini golf, video games, saw a movie, all the fun stuff. We took time to visit the Science center. I cooked a turkey dinner on Thanksgiving. Oh, how I loved to cook for my boy and watch him eat! I will cherish that visit always as the gift that it was, the last one before he got his test results back before Christmas.

The spot on the back of his tongue was Squamous Cell Carcinoma, which comprises over 95% of oropharyngeal cancers. Tobacco and alcohol are major risk factors. Colton was not a heavy drinker. Colton was a non-smoker. He was 25 years old. Why!? We were not sure what to expect, but it was not that. Not in a million years.

In early January of 2017, Colton was flown to Vancouver B.C. by a program called Angel Air. He underwent a surgery to remove the Cancer and surrounding tissue. He did very well with the surgery and was happy to hear that they were confident that they were able to remove it all. Within a few weeks, Colton was flown to Vancouver a second time to remove more tissue, collectively the size of a thumb from his tongue. He was given exercises to do, so that his speech would not be affected, and he did them faithfully. During the procedure, a neck excision was done, and several lymph nodes were removed for testing. The Cancer had spread to 4 of them. Now Colton's journey was well under way.

A side note that must be mentioned: during this time, my mother was nearing the end of her life journey. It was 2 years to the week that my father had died. I was unable to spend the time that I felt I should have with her, but any vacation time and extra money belonged to my one and only child. For me, the choice was simple and clear. I had to focus on Colton. All I could do was hope that on some level she understood. She and I had always had a tumultuous relationship. A combination of never being able to live up to her expectations, and of me being the one that she chose to talk to about all her hopes and aspirations. She was a true romantic at heart. If we had met as friends instead of mother/daughter, we may have gotten along quite well. In my quieter moments, I sometimes hope that she is watching me write, or seeing a finished painting, and is wearing a smile. Those were 2 of her passions. At the base layer of the onion, there was real love. I am beyond grateful that my sister and brother were able to be there for her during that time. It was a time of separation. Sorting vastly different grief into neat little compartments of the mind to be dealt with later. Oh, the silly little lies we tell ourselves...

Chapter 4

That Horrible Phone Call

By this time, Randy and I were transferred again to Cochrane Alberta, approximately 30 minutes from Calgary. I remember feeling so far away and out of the loop with much of the information and what was happening at that time. I know that this was a combination of Colton not knowing how to explain all the medical terms and procedures and partly him wanting to protect me. I just know that there were not enough trips back to Prince George. All I could do was keep sending money to keep them afloat as Colton was now having to start his rounds of chemotherapy and radiation and was unable to work. He would tell me later that he did not like who he became when he was taking the chemotherapy medication. He became angry and abusive, lashing out at his girlfriend and friends. He said he felt like a drug addict, that it completely changed his personality. I remember finding this so hard to believe as my son had the sweetest disposition and rarely even used foul language.

By the summer of 2017 he had finished his medical treatment and was given the "all clear" from his

Oncology team. Even though he was still weak he went back to work and slowly his life seemed to return to normal. I breathed a huge sigh of relief and planned a visit that fall and requested that we have some family pictures taken in the local park where Randy and I were married. My best friend Barb is an avid photographer and took some lovely photos of us.

By October, Colton started having extreme back pain and wondered if he had lifted something and pulled a muscle. He was an auto glass installer, so this was a possibility. He had gone for some routine tests and was awaiting the results.

Randy and I were in Mexico for a week in early November. I knew he was waiting for test results on Monday, and we would be home by then, so I was not worried. However, he got his results early. The Cancer had returned and spread. He was given the news that his condition was terminal. He was given this news while I, his mother, was out of the country! In his initial moments of despair, this fact had escaped him, and he called everyone he could think of to try and reach me. My friend Barb knew which hotel we were at, and he was able to contact me. Whenever I think of this call, it happens in slow motion. I remember him saying "Mom, I'm fucked!

It is in my lungs, liver, spine, and skull." All I could say was "I am on my way. I love you. I am on my way." The breakdown that followed was something rarely seen in the lobby of a fancy resort, but all I noticed was that everyone was moved to the far end of the lobby reception desk. Once Randy got me back to our room, I called Barb. All I kept saying was "How will I endure this? How will I endure this?" And all she kept saying was "I don't know, I don't know..." I do not remember much of that last day before our flight back to Canada. It was a mere 24 hours between getting home, repacking and boarding my flight back to Prince George.

Chapter 5

By His Side

Things happened so quickly from that moment on. Colton's girlfriend picked me up at the airport. I briefly thought that I had never seen her look like that before. The lack of sleep and overwhelming stress was more than evident. We drove straight to the hospital, as Colton was already too weak to handle being at home and needed more care than his girlfriend could provide on her own.

I remember being so relieved and happy to see him and at the same time it felt like a punch in the throat. All he wanted was for me to be there. I could see the relief in those beautiful blue eyes when I told him I was not going anywhere. He looked haggard. Frail and thin, depressed, tired. One of the first conversations that we had, there in the Emergency room, was how he would rather be dead than go back to the job that he had at the time. It had been a source of stress since he had started there, and his boss was very demanding, often leaving Colton to believe that he was not living up to his expectations. He was clearly overwhelmed at this point. All of us were, and this was just the beginning. I could not believe that he was even thinking of work at that moment, not to mention that he was talking about dying! What was happening? But he had a deep sense of responsibility and was already worrying about all the details of his life that had to be worked out now. He was deeply stressed and overloaded, scared and traumatized by all of it. We had previously spoken about he and his girlfriend coming to live with us in Cochrane for the remainder of his days, and we had the ok from the doctors to do so if his medications could make it possible for him to fly unaided, not by air ambulance. Everything had been arranged. All he wanted was to be with me. Now it was plain to see that this was no longer an option. But, as soon as I told him that I would be by his side from now on, he seemed to relax. I had a difficult phone call with my employer, who also had an only son. I took an open-ended leave of absence. Compassionate Leave. This was my job now, and I really had no idea what the coming days and weeks would bring.

A Letter to my brother, November 30, 2017: Colton Update:

Hi bro, here is a brief update.

The Dr. does not want to move him to Cochrane, but it is Colton's wish to be with me so he is trying to get his meds regulated so that he can manage without an IV. He will be on a Fentanyl patch and pills for the pain management, and we have contacted our doctor in Cochrane already.

We are hoping for this to happen in a week or so. The oncologist told us he thinks he has several months left. He is starting to eat more so he is gaining a bit of energy so that is good. The GoFundMe page has raised $6500 so far so that will help. Also, there is an event planned at the pub by their place on the 17th with a silent auction, 50/50 etc. Thankfully, he has loan protector insurance on his debt, so he is in effect debt free, as this is important to him. He has signed a DNR. I have a copy in my wallet. He and his girlfriend will have a small ceremony to marry once we are settled, she wants that so bad. The Cancer is the same Squamous Cell Carcinoma but has spread to his lung, ribs, vertebrae, liver and now skull. It is not in his brain. Although he is short tempered on occasion he is "all there" and wants family around. His father and stepmom left to go home today but I will be staying to fly back to Cochrane with him, so it had better be soon. They gave notice to be out of their rental by the end of the month. Randy will take back whatever he can when he heads back in a day or two. Work is so crazy heading into Christmas, I cannot believe I am not there. Honestly, I cannot believe any of this. Randy says this is just another river of shit that we must cross, but for me, there is just a world without Colton on the other side of it. The body has an endless supply of tears, and the heart can beat while continually breaking. This is fucking unfair. No one should have to be in such pain or to witness their child trying to endure it. Love you, Nancy.

Colton never made it back home to Cochrane with us. He stayed 2 weeks in hospital, 2 weeks at his rental place, 2 weeks in Hospice. Was this a gift, that he was taken so quickly? My mind says yes as he was suffering so, but my heart says no, no, no...

The events that took place during my 6 weeks with Colton were the hardest part of the story to write. Some reasons being obvious, as describing the things my son endured is such a personal and private thing. Even describing the depths of emotion that I was trying to process during that time is still being unpacked in my heart and mind, 6 years later. But it goes something like this:

Chapter 6

Loving Support

I had no idea how much support I would need during this time. I did not know how much support Colton would need. There were many days where I felt like I indeed knew truly little about anything. However, I had my best friend, Barb. Honestly, she saved me. She was a gift to me during this time, as she continues to be to this day. She is my soul sister. When I frantically repacked and flew to Prince George, I had no idea what to take or how long I would be gone. I only knew I was going to stay with Barb. She would have it no other way. It was not a question. Her home would be my home base. There was such comfort in that knowledge. This was unfamiliar territory. We did not know at the time that this would mean some 54 days... To say that my arrival and Colton's situation disrupted her (and her hubby Dave's) life was a huge understatement! The first 2 weeks, Colton was in the hospital, ending in palliative care. What?? How could this be happening? I was in shock. We all were. His girlfriend was a mess. Exhausted. Emotional. Colton was often angry, then apologetic, and very weak. I was often quiet, in disbelief, trying to figure everything out, trying to take care of anything that I could take care of. The hospital was overcrowded, as always, but somehow, they found Colton a private room, and later found a foldout couch so that we could take turns staying with him. The nurses were so compassionate! I could see that they were invested in this dying young man's comfort. I am thankful for that. I am thankful for a great many things that happened during that time that I was not acknowledging enough. I was just operating on instinct. I bought groceries, snacks, and lots of wine. I brought him cut up watermelon, smoothies, or cookies or whatever he wanted when he felt like he could eat.

I feel like I want to mention this. One time when I was out getting groceries, I ran into the mother of Randy's sons. We had never been friends, but this encounter was so different. We stood and looked at each other, on the verge of tears. I always was. I was unprepared for this, but she took me in her arms and hugged me. I needed one. I am sure that she knew somehow that it just as easily could have been one of her boys. That she was the lucky one who did not have to endure this. She knew my son, who he was. This was uncalled for. No one, let alone Colton, deserved to go out this way, suffering while Cancer ate you alive, I am grateful for that meeting.

I remember one night in particular. It was my turn to stay overnight in his hospital room, so his girlfriend could hopefully go home and sleep. Colton and I talked a little, but he was heavily medicated and slept off and on. In the middle of the night, he was awake after the nurse came in to check his vitals. I asked if I could get him anything. He said eggnog. Weird, I know, but it was that time of year and eggnog mixed half and half with milk was his favorite. So, I went to the little fridge out past the nurse's station and spoke with the nurse on duty briefly as I took Colton's snacks and prepared a little picnic for us. I microwaved a chocolate chip cookie, grabbed the cut-up watermelon, whatever I could find. I saw that the nurse was near tears, as was I. She came out from behind the desk and gave me a big hug. Here I was, just a mom fixing a snack for her son. I went in and sat on his bed, and he started to eat. He had barely eaten all day because he was so nauseous. He enjoyed the warm, melty cookie, smiled at me, and said, "This is what I needed. I needed someone who knows what I need." I cannot tell you how much those words meant to me, and I am bawling my head off as I type this, because oh my god do I miss moments like that! So, so much. The kicker to this story, however, is that when I reminded him of it the next day, he had no recollection of our picnic, or the conversation we had. I remember how sad I was at that moment, but now, I am simply grateful that on some level, he was able to tell me that he needed his momma.

Mostly, I sat beside my son. I was simply there to bear witness to what he was enduring. The medications, the tests, the I.V. needles that he hated. The nausea. The inability to eat. He said everything tasted like metal. This was a side effect of the medication, and he would rinse his mouth with mouthwash over and over to try and get rid of the taste. He started to put pepper sauce on everything and that helped for a while. The struggle. Those first few days are frustrating for me to sort through, even now, 6 years later. There was so much to figure out. There were medications to be regulated. Courses of treatment that were tried and then abandoned. The stuff of his life that he insisted on being thoroughly handled. I watched my son get his affairs in order. I cannot express how huge of a thing this was for me to watch. This was not supposed to be happening. He planned who he would gift his favorite belongings to. He sold his beloved truck. All the things that he had worked so hard for. He paid his debts. He showed me without question what a fine man he had become. I was and am so incredibly proud of him. This indeed was a gift that I will always cherish.

On the evenings that I did not sleep in Colton's hospital room, I stayed at Barb's and she and I would have a glass of wine and talk about everything. We would cry together. She held space for me and let me cry out the day. She is an empath. This situation was a huge emotional draw on her as well. There were days she could not go to work as this was taking such a toll on her. She made sure I was given the option to eat, and a place to sleep when I could stay awake no longer. She was my angel on earth, and I am forever grateful. Sometimes, there are times in your life that you are not equipped to deal with it on your own. You will have to have help to get through these times. If you have someone like my Barb to help you through, you are truly blessed. One special thing that Barb did for me during this time, and there were many, was to take photos. I cannot express what this has meant to me over the years, as there are many moments that were documented for me. Thank you so much, my dear friend. Her selflessness and love carried me through the toughest days, and the hospitality shown by Barb and Dave to Randy, and I will never be forgotten.

My husband Randy was making trips back and forth from Alberta, over the Rocky Mountains in December, dragging our travel trailer to have a private space when needed, as he managed his time with work in the middle of the chaos. He was worried sick about being away from me and I was worried sick about his treacherous trips back and forth during this time. He did not speak much of his own feelings, as he did not want to burden me. He lent me his strength and gave me his love, which was so sorely needed during that time. And of course, today. There is no way to measure the value of this kind of emotional support.

I am grateful to our Cochrane friends and the team at his store there for supporting him during that time. You all are forever in our hearts.

Chapter 7

Taking Control (of letting go)

Soon, Colton made some decisions about his medical care. At the time, he was being treated for an infection in his lung and had to get a new I.V. put in every day as his veins were not cooperating. He had always hated getting needles more than anything, and he had his full share of them all his life. I remember him angrily saying (in a bit of a rant) "Is all this going to cure the Cancer? No? Then I am done with it! Why put me through this?" We could not argue with logic like that.

One moment stands out for me during this time. I was following his wheelchair as he was being taken for a scan. I saw the chart on the back of his wheelchair. In someone's beautiful penmanship it read "Let die a natural death." I remember having to swallow the urge to cry, scream and throw up in that moment so that he would not know. It was a punch in the face, and I certainly was never meant to see that. Even now as I type this, the feeling sits heavy on my heart. What was "natural" about any of this? This scan resulted in a brief meeting between me and the oncologist confirming that Colton would not be receiving any further chemotherapy treatment. The time for healing had long passed. Now the goal was comfort and peace.

It continues to be my personal goal as well. During this time, I was moved to see how many visitors Colton had in the hospital. I mean, people do not like spending time in hospitals, as a rule. But they showed up daily for my son. There were many that I did not know, but I would soon know all their names, and how they knew my son. Many were glad to finally meet Colton's "momma," which made me smile.

There was a visit from my 2 nephews, who drove down from northern B.C. to visit Colton. They were strong and humble enough to put aside the rules of their religious upbringing to say goodbye to their cousin and visit me, who was no longer a part of their faith. It had been many, many years since I had seen them, and the visit meant a great deal to us both. It is during the most difficult of times when family is needed most. The need is ongoing, as many hands make the work lighter, and grief is such heavy work.

And one, Randy's eldest son, Bailey, spent a great deal of time keeping Colton company. He is a quiet man. He did not say much. But his constant effort and consistent presence meant the world to us. I know they had a close bond. Like brothers without the 'step.' It became evident to me during that time and earned a place in my weary heart.

It was shortly after this that Colton was to have palliative care at home since he would not be having any further treatment at the hospital. I remember this scaring the crap out of me. No 'round the clock care? No nurse to check on him every night? At that time, there were no available rooms at the Hospice House in Prince George. Until that was an option, we got busy getting their rental place ready for him. Their landlord had agreed for them to stay as long as needed considering the circumstances, which was a gift at the time. A hospital bed was brought in. We purchased a wonderfully comfortable lift chair, and a rolling side table for his pain meds. In-home nursing visits were arranged. I remember being shocked at the sheer number of bottles of medications that covered the kitchen island. Colton was wearing several Fentanyl patches at once to manage the pain. Looking back, it was amazing that this amount of medication only took the edge off his pain so that he could visit with us, get up and slowly get himself to the bathroom, eat tiny amounts of the foods I prepared. It enabled him to cope as best as he could during this time. I even learned how to bake cookies laced with Cannabis to help him relax and cope with the pain and anxiety. I am quite sure that at one point or another, these were sampled by all of us. I spent as much time as I could with him during this time, but I stayed overnight with Barb at her house, as Colton's extended family as well as his girlfriend's family began to arrive. To the best of my ability, I tried to remind them that Colton needed a lot of rest and quiet at this time, unless he said something different. Often, my time there with him consisted of him reclining in his lift chair, eyes closed, listening to the Nature channel as he found this relaxing and meditative. This should have been the time for me to have deeper conversations and ask questions about what was happening to him, his wishes, his fears...but it did not happen. I learned what to ask and what not to ask. I got yelled at. I got hugged and told how much I was loved. I experienced every emotion. Then, in the evening, Barb would pour the wine and cry with me.

During this time, my sister flew to Prince George to spend some time with us and to see her nephew for the last time. She and her family also made a monetary donation to his GoFundMe which was truly needed and appreciated. It was wonderful to have a member of my family there, to talk to, to cry with, to share what I was going through. As with so many things in life, you just had to be there. Again, it is when you need your family the most.

Also, in the middle of December, in the middle of a snowstorm, Colton and his girlfriend exchanged vows in a brief ceremony. The photos show my son, in his suit which once fit him so well, now hanging off his rail thin body. The rest of us looked tired, awkward. There was a photo of Colton with his father and I on either side of him. I know that he cherished that photo. My thoughts about the lack of necessity to have put him through that kind of stress in the last weeks of his life are, and forever will be, summed up in this one statement.

There was a part of Colton's life that needs to be a part of this story. The last 6 years of his life gave him a special bond of friendship with a group of musicians in a local death metal band in Prince George. Colton would go to all their shows. At first, he was hesitant to tell me about it, as some of the shows were in rather sketchy areas of Prince George and he did not want me to worry about him. Also, it was death metal, the connotations of which were, well, scary. But he assured me that he was being responsible and that this was a cool bunch of guys. I remember him being so excited when he told me that one time as the band was doing a sound check, he was making some vocals into the microphone. The rest of the band was blown away and he had earned their appreciation for his ability to throat sing/growl as they do in that genre of music. I am not sure how to describe it, but he used to scare me with that 'monster voice' since he was a little kid, running up behind me and grabbing me, as little monsters do. This talent earned Colton the role of lead vocalist in the band, and he told me that travelling and performing with them were some of the happiest years of his life. I am thankful that I have some of his performance photos on my wall, which are truly awesome, and for the outpouring of love for Colton from this amazing group of young men.

The band was something that, unfortunately, Colton could never share with his father, as that would have been shunned by the religion/belief system that he had at the time. He and his father would never have had a relationship past the age of 15 when his father sold everything and left town with his new wife, except that Colton conscientiously made the effort to hop a bus (or eventually drive) and go to see his father every year to try and maintain their relationship. He would cut his hair, shave off his beard, wear a generic t-shirt instead of his favorite metal band shirts, and totally pretend to be someone that he was not, someone that his father would approve of. I obviously found this to be unnecessary, and we had a few conversations about it over the years. It was never my place to tell his father about this. I hoped that the rules of his religion would hopefully never affect the love a father has for his son. Colton was so afraid that his father would shun him. But, once you had Colton's love, you just had it. At the end, it seemed that much of the city was aware of Colton and his position in the band, and the community events in his honor were on the radio. His father heard it. So, then he knew. Colton was completely freaked out about this when it happened, but thankfully, his father just said that he thought it was cool to be in a band. Honestly, what else was he supposed to say as his son was dying and the community was rallying around him? I am grateful for the fact that Colton remained loved and accepted by him during those last few weeks. The relief that he felt was obvious, and it broke my heart that he had carried this worry needlessly for 6 years.

There was more than one community event to help support Colton at this time. A pub night that included a silent auction with items donated by community members, including Barb's hubby Dave, who painted a beautiful canvas honoring Colton, a 50/50 draw, food specials, even a concert. Extended family members and friends were a tremendous help during this time. Colton's stepsister Michelle was instrumental in organizing the events, the GoFundMe, cooking meals in Hospice, getting a video and equipment ready for the memorial, so many things that I am sure I do not know about. I love this woman so much. So did Colton.

A memory that stands out during this time was how excited Colton was that the new Star Wars movie, The Last Jedi, was about to be released. He had always been such a huge fan. We had tried every avenue possible to get a streamed copy of the film in case he did not make it to see it at the theater. As it turned out, we were able to go to see it, all of us as a blended family. Colton sat next to me, and I watched him watch the film. A scene where Luke leaves his body behind and rejoins the force made me cry and put a special look on my son's face. The next day, unfortunately, left him devastated as he remembered nothing of the experience due to his pain medication.

Then came Christmas. Seriously?! Honestly, I could not have cared less. Yet here we were, invading our friends' home during the holidays! It was unthinkable! It was the worst of times, and we were trying our very hardest to find a shred of something...joy? No. It cannot be Christmas. Not now. There was no joy to be found, at least for me. Barb's hubby had been laid off from work. I was off work and had not been paid for quite some time. Yet somehow, somehow, we managed presents, meals, family gatherings, the whole thing. That was a miracle. Knowing that this was Barb's favorite holiday made my heart ache even more. But I was able to cook one last Christmas turkey for my son. Of course, he ate little, but I caught him watching me more than once. We both knew this was the last one. We never spoke of it. But those looks said it all. Oh my god my heart! That was a gift. I must call it a gift, or it will tear me wide open yet again, and nobody needs to see that. F'ing grief.

I have cooked turkeys since then. It has never felt the same. Christmas has never felt the same. That is what loss does. That is what grief does. It changes everything.

Chapter 8

Hospice

By the end of the year, it was time to take Colton to Hospice. I thought this would be the worst news possible, but soon found it to be a comfort, knowing that he would have round-the-clock care and his pain would be managed properly there. Also, there was a couch that folded down, so someone always stayed with him in the room, which was vital. Also, there were a couple of living room/gathering areas, so everyone could visit without having to all crowd into his room. There was also a large kitchen facility so we could take turns making dinner there.

I cannot say enough about the Prince George Hospice House and the wonderful people that work there. They know and understand grief. That is the understatement of the century.

Once we had Colton all settled into his room, I felt a sense of calm about him that I had not seen or felt up to that point. He was becoming increasingly frustrated, though, at how his body was beginning to shut down. The simple task of going to the bathroom unaided was becoming an issue, as well as his lack of strength. But he was softening. His anger was nearly gone.

During this time, my brother drove up from Kelowna for a visit. He and Colton had a special bond. They had a good visit at the Hospice House. Colton always trusted him and confided in him, and I am forever grateful for the love and support he extended to us during that time. That visit over New Years' and all his support since then has truly been a lifesaver. It meant so much to me that another member of my family was there to support me, Randy, and Colton.

Colton's heart was touched at that time by a lasting gift. One of his best friends and his wife had just had their second child, a boy, on New Year's Day. They had given his middle name to be Colton, out of love for my son. How wonderful is that? The New Year's baby makes the front page of the local paper, and the story of his name lets the whole city know about Colton and his battle with Cancer. His friends brought the baby to Hospice for Colton to hold and photos to be taken. It melted my heart to see the look of love and wonder on his face.

I have some regrets about my time spent at the Hospice with Colton. I know that regrets serve no purpose. It is more of a disappointment. You see, a great deal of my time was taken up preparing food for all of Colton's friends and family, and not enough spent with him. I believe, in hindsight, that I was simply keeping busy and doing what any mother would do in my situation given the chance, which was to prepare all my son's favorite dishes one last time. There just was not enough time for all the conversations. I was certainly not the only one preparing food, Colton's stepmom and stepsister were an integral part of this as well, and I am eternally grateful for them and their love for Colton. He had decided to try and connect with as many of his friends as possible to say goodbye. He had put an open invitation on Facebook to all the friends he went to school with. He attended school from kindergarten through grade 12 in Prince George, so that equaled a lot of friends. They came. So many of them came. The ones that could not come, or had moved away, made video calls. As a result, between school friends and musician friends, the Hospice turned out to be quite a busy time. I am not angry about this. I am grateful for this, for Colton's sake. Even though it was physically taxing for him, he sat and listened to stories, laughed at the jokes, and let them take group photos. They played music, they sang, they ate with him. I know that Colton saw this as a gift. He saw how much he was loved and appreciated. I just wanted more time. Of course. It is a selfish statement, and it is true. When I saw that he was pushing himself and becoming exhausted, I put a sign by the entrance limiting his visitors to family. It was necessary. If you are reading this and you are faced with a comparable situation, do your future grieving self a favor and do not feel that you must take care of everything. Do not feel like you must cook enough to feed the entire community. Spend this most crucial time with the most important person, your loved one. Remember, the goal is to have no regrets.

Eventually, for the last several days or so, Randy and I were given a suite to stay in at the Hospice House since we were there from out of province. This was truly a gift as it gave us a private space to begin to grieve together, and more time with Colton. It also gave our friends Barb and Dave a much-needed break from us as well. It was deeply appreciated. For times when others were with Colton, we spent our time looking at properties for sale in Campbell River B.C. From the moment we had been transferred from Prince George to Alberta, we had been trying to get back to Randy's hometown. We visited every year, spending vacation weeks at his family's lakeside vacation property, and along the way, I fell in love with the island. At this point it was still a dream we shared. Originally, we had a plan to make sure we had a basement suite for Colton and his girlfriend, but sadly some dreams just did not come true.

One morning in Hospice it was just Colton and I having breakfast together. Cherished time. He was solemn and thoughtful. He said "Mom, this morning I woke up to someone crying and saying, 'I missed it.' I said "Well honey, many people wait until their loved ones are out of the room before they pass. They go to get coffee or go pee and when they come back it is too late. They think that they are saving them from the pain of seeing them go." He looked at me and nodded, deep in thought. I looked him right in the eyes and said, "Don't be that guy." He said to me "I'll see what I can do, Mom."

I spent hours and hours holding his hand. Both in the hospital and in Hospice. I had Randy sneak a few photos of our hands so that I could remember how they looked and felt. At first, in the hospital, he did not want me to take photos and would get angry about everything. But later, in Hospice, he did not mind. Most of his anger was gone. His true sweet personality shone back through, and he was full of love, laughter, and kindness for all his family, friends, and visitors. He would make the effort to get up and walk over and wrap his arms around me and say, "love you Momma." He always tickled a little on my back with his fingers. His signature thing. I would move heaven and earth to feel him do that again.

Chapter 9

Colton's Decision

Colton had some conversations with his doctor and his hospice nurse that no one was invited to. He made some big decisions. He decided to ask for MAID, medical assistance in dying.

For this to be made possible, the patient must be of a sound mind, and answer a series of questions, explaining in detail the degree of pain and suffering he has endured. There were a panel of at least 2 doctors and 2 nurses present.

Colton proceeded to explain in graphic detail that his terminal Cancer had progressed to the point where he felt like he was 90 years old. He described in detail that he was unable to go to the bathroom anymore, that he was unable to have sex anymore, that he was in constant unbearable pain. His heart wrenching speech is something a mother could never forget. The panel of doctors and nurses agreed with Colton's decision, however, there was just one problem: at the time (2018) this took place, Colton would have to be transported to the hospital and have the drugs administered there. This was a huge disappointment for him, as he did not want to leave

Hospice. He felt a level of comfort and safety there. The alternative was for him to be sedated, and he opted for this.

At first, Colton only invited his two sets of parents to discuss this with. Then slowly he told the other family and close friends that were present. Then, he proceeded to do something that I will never forget as long as I remain on this earth.

With significant effort, he got up, walked over to each person in the room, gave them a hug, thanked them, and told them he loved them. He saved me for last. I got my last hug and kiss, and "and I love you the most." There was a soft chuckle or two and he started to say, "I love you all the same" but I quickly said "nope, I heard you and I'm taking it." or something close to those words...it was such an intense moment. I have never been prouder of my son, and the mature, loving, sensitive man that he had become.

It was a Friday night. We had a copy of the Star Wars movie. I was sitting on his left side of the bed, and his bride was on his right. They started the movie, and he was given sedation meds. We watched for a few moments. His eyes were closed. Some space weapons were being fired. He said, "you all hear that? Pew. Pew..." someone laughed and said "yeah, we hear it." As his head fell backwards, I grabbed a pillow and placed it underneath his head just in time. I heard Randy say "ah, nice catch, Momma."

After that, it took a little time to get the level of sedation exactly right. Then came the wait. We were informed that it could take a few days. His body was failing, but his heart was strong, and he was only 26 years old.

Of course, there was no way I could sleep that night. His bed was surrounded. I sat and held his hand in silence. All night. One by one, each of the faces around the bed slowly put their head down and went to sleep and began to snore. I did not blame them. It was both physical and emotional exhaustion. But I sat. I kept vigil all night long. I could feel everything changing. My joy, my happiness. I could feel it leaving my body. Truthfully, the next couple of days went by in a blur. I honestly do not remember what I did. I finally slept in small amounts. I visited with whoever was there, but I truly cannot remember.

On Monday morning, Colton's stepsister Michelle had to fly home to Vancouver. She spent some time with Colton to say goodbye. She told me that she had let him know that he could go whenever he was ready.

That evening, Colton's dad and stepmother were in his room reading. I was sitting in the kitchen on my iPad looking at houses for sale while Randy and Bailey played a crib game. It was shortly after 8pm and I wanted to say goodnight to Colton and check in before going to bed. I told Randy this and then headed to Colton's room.

My life was about to change forever, and Colton was about to keep his promise.

Chapter 10

A Promise Kept

I walked into the room to find Colton's dad and stepmom on the couch reading. I went to Colton's bedside and noticed that his forehead and upper lip had beads of sweat on them. This was different, like he was struggling. I went into his bathroom and soaked a cloth with cold water to wash his face, and as I walked back toward the bed, his breathing changed. It went from the short raspy breaths to a couple of long, relaxed breaths. I said, "did you hear that? His breathing changed." I rushed to Colton and began to wipe the damp cloth over his face. As I did, I watched the color drain from his beautiful face until his lips were grey.

I heard my voice, but it did not sound like me. It said "are you leaving me honey? Are you leaving me now? I love you. Thank you for waiting, thank you for waiting for me." In the background I could hear his stepmom crying and saying over and over "he waited for his mommy, he waited for his mommy" I am not sure how many times we each repeated this. Many. Of course, there was much going on in the background that I was unaware of at the time. Time had stopped for me. But now I know that Randy had been told to hurry to the room, saw it was happening, then had gone to find Colton's bride and her father, and that other people were called. I neither saw nor remember any of this. What happened next was like a dream. It was like nothing else that I had ever experienced before or since.

I could not take my eyes off Colton's face. His left eye, the one that was affected by that horrible infection all those years ago, did not close all the way. I touched it gently. I touched his hair and his cheek. I was mumbling, like a mantra, repeating the phrase for a while, "thank you for waiting, I love you, thank you for waiting", eventually lowering my head to him. I could not make out what was being said behind me, for Colton had wrapped me in a cocoon of sound. It was a higher pitched vibration, like an old vacuum whirring in my head and it was as if there was a bubble around us, as if he were taking me with him for a part of his journey in a capsule of his own making. It was utterly amazing. It was all encompassing. It was a gift from him to me, to protect me in the moment. I am certain of it. I stayed there with him until the sound faded and eventually, I could hear other sounds in the room again. Much, much later I would ask Randy how long this had lasted. I had suggested that it was 10 or 15 minutes.

He shook his head with a small smile and said that no, it had been for an hour. Colton had loaned me a blanket of peace, so that I was able to endure the moment, a gift that I am eternally grateful for. I remember crawling up on his bed and lying beside him. From there I could see the others in the room, but I did not speak. His doctor had arrived and stood at a distance. We locked our eyes at one point and neither of us had to say anything. There are no words for this moment. There was no way to prepare for something like this, even though you knew it was coming. I cannot recall how much time had passed, but the room eventually cleared out, with people moving to the gathering/living room area. Then there was just Colton, his wife and me. We had taken the task of bathing and dressing Colton away from the nurses. In hindsight, I have no idea how we managed to do this.

Very calmly, peacefully, we began this final gesture of love. Now I know that we were both in shock, but then, it had just seemed like the most natural thing we could have done for him. We spoke a few words during this time, but I do not remember what they were. We slowly and thoroughly washed him and put on his favorite black metal band t-shirt and a pair of black sweatpants. This is what he wore most days.

This is what he had chosen. I know there is a gap here but the next thing I remember I am back in his room, and Randy has his arms around me. Colton is on a stretcher, on top of a body bag, but it is open. The room has people. The other set of parents, his wife, and her father. Others. All I remember hearing was the voice of the nurse, "Are you ready for us to close the bag?" I do not remember answering. There was a pause. Did I give a slight nod? Then it was done, and I would never see that face again, except in photos, and dreams, and in my mind from that moment on.

Things happened in slow motion. They left the room with him. I followed out into the hallway. I received hugs and tears and condolences from the nurses and staff on duty. I saw the candle burning on the mantel in the entrance. There was a card with his name propped in front of it. I had seen other names in front of the candle in the previous days and weeks of our stay there. Somehow, I never imagined seeing the name Colton on the card.

I remember there was a moment of "what do we do now?" Randy and I went to the little suite at the back of the Hospice House and packed up our things and drove to Barb and Dave's place. There, we settled in for an extraordinarily long night. Long, comforting hugs from my best friend. I did my best to comfort her too, as we were all grieving together. My husband held my head as I wept. I wonder if he had any idea how often he would do this for me in the coming days. The days that turn into years that turn into our future. A future full of change. A future without Colton. With that, Monday, January 15, 2018, changed me forever.

It was so terrifying for me to revisit this part repeatedly. I procrastinated for so long after I got to that part of the story. After reading, crying, editing, and more crying, I am all wrung out, but only for a moment, for it seems there is an endless supply of tears. You could almost believe that was the end of the story, right? But I was to find out that my work had just begun.

Chapter 11

The Obituary and Celebration of Life.

Things began to speed up after that day. I remember that Barb and I were able to spend time together, and oh my god, I needed that. Since Colton's wishes were to be cremated, we spent some time thinking about how they were to be distributed and what I would be taking mine home in. Even typing that sentence just feels so very wrong on every level. I am sitting here writing this 6 years later and I still, for the life of me, cannot comprehend coming to terms with this. The grey/white powdery remains of my one and only child, split between his father, his wife, and me. Unbelievable, yet it happened.

We found a place in town that had small charms that could hold ashes and be worn on a necklace. I purchased one for myself and one for his wife. I did not want an urn. I do not believe it was ever my intent to keep the ashes forever. Even in that moment, I understood that he was not in there. I found a beautiful tin and that worked fine. Barb and I went to a psychic medium during this time, and once again later. We were intrigued by the things she had to say.

We each bought a set of angel cards. Thus began a spiritual journey that continued for both of us.

An obituary needed to be written and a hall rented for a gathering to honor Colton to take place. Amazingly, a hall was available a mere 3 days later. The notice in the paper would not wait.

I insisted on being the one who wrote it. Today looking back, I have absolutely no idea how I accomplished this task. Up to this point, I was in a whirlwind of sorts, with all this grief and emotion, people, decisions, and tears swirling around me. It was and is a complete feeling of helplessness. I will not rewrite the obit here because of the extended family names and such, for the same reason as only a select few names have been used in this book at all. For the names not mentioned are no longer in contact with me. Colton was the bond that kept us in each other's lives, and that bond is no more. I am certain that this happens often, not just to me. All I know is that I wanted to make Colton proud. I wanted to include everyone that needed to be mentioned and to say things about my son that I knew were important to him. As we had to leave the province and go home quite soon after the service, that date of the Celebration of Life turned out to be the day after the obit was published. Even so, the hall was filled with people who love Colton. There were many people there that I did not know, as they were from the other side of the extended family, or friends of Colton's from school, or the boys from the band that Colton was a part of. More than enough food showed up without my knowledge or input of any kind. I remember thinking later "who planned all this?" because clearly, I was not in a state to have done it. It was coordinated by his stepsister, her family, and others who loved Colton, and for which I am truly thankful. Michelle had stepped in from the beginning and set up the community events that were such a success. Though we did not know each other prior to his illness, she and I bonded over our love for Colton and our similar spiritual beliefs. She is a gift that I treasure, and I am eternally grateful for all her help during this time.

Somehow, even in those dark moments, when important decisions needed to be made, as his mother, I made them. At the core of a mother's heart, there is a strength to do anything that needs to be done for her child. At the service, I was told that someone wanted to get up and say a few words, and did I wish to go first? Up to that moment, I had no intention of speaking. Looking back, this is surprising to me because of course people get up and speak at funerals. For some reason I simply had not thought of it. So, I took a "time out" and sat in the lobby of the hall for a while and wrote a speech. It went something like this:

On this special day I want to thank everyone that is here this evening for the love and support that they have shown to my one and only child. Since I have been here, back in Prince George, I have seen an outpouring of love from all that know Colton, from high school friends to local musicians to family to co-workers and people in the community that know him. This young man has touched so many lives and is loved by many. As a mother, I see there is no better testament to the man that he has become than to see him surrounded by love at this time. Today, everyone here has become one family. I am also so proud of him today, for he has chosen a wife to share his life, who no one here could have chosen better. I love her like my own daughter. So, Colton, to quote the only astronaut we knew, "I love you To Eternity and Beyond."

I want to mention, with reference to Colton's wife, that she was his primary caregiver from the moment he found out he had Cancer. She took on this task with a fierce love and determination like I have never seen in such a young woman. Colton loved her so much. They had been married for less than a month. She has since moved on and has children of her own now, and though she no longer contacts me, I see through social media that she is doing well. In respect of that fact, I have not referred to her by name. We grieve in our own way. Grief is as individual and unique as you are.

When Colton was little and the first Toy Story movie came out, I bought him the Buzz Lightyear toy that made noise and said "To Eternity... And beyond!" Sometimes, instead of "I love you more," it would be "to Eternity and Beyond." I also note that in reference to the speech, I only referred to Colton in the present tense. To me, he was not gone. I mean who would not want to hang around long enough to attend their own Celebration of Life, to see who showed up and what they had to say? I know I would.

I know that he would have been so pleased, even overwhelmed to see a community hall filled with people who knew and loved him. What a gift!

There were 3 distinctly different sections of people there: His father, along with that side of the family were of a different faith, and there were many there that I did not know. Even though Colton was not of that faith, they came to support that side of the family and I was glad that they did.

There were quite a large group of Colton's Death Metal bandmates and friends from that area of his life. Although Colton did not look like this long-haired, tattooed group of men, he, as their lead vocalist, was so loved by them that they showed up in droves. The lead guitarist got up to speak and told some funny anecdotes about Colton, his love for his friends, that he was a 'momma's boy,' and how much he loved my roast beef and loaded mashed potatoes. They referred to him as 'brother,' which I know he loved as he was an only child.

Then there were the rest of us. Randy and I, his 2 sons and their mom, Barb, and Dave, Colton's bride with her family, school friends, and coworkers. I am sure he was right there, checking out the slide show, the table with the display of photos, cards, flowers, and candles, and of course, the food.

In hindsight, I am so grateful that I did write his Obituary. I am so grateful that I got up first to speak at his gathering. I would encourage bereaved parents to do the same or participate in whatever way you have the strength to, because you will not regret it. You will not get another chance. It is a gift you can still give to your child. There are many tasks at that time that are extremely hard. Burial or cremation? What will you put the ashes in? Do you want a necklace to hold some of the ashes? I hope you have/had someone special and close to you to talk through these things with and who will help you make these important decisions. I am grateful that I did. If you can, have these difficult conversations while you have time. I am glad that Colton had the opportunity and the presence of mind to make his own decision about choosing to be cremated. I do have a necklace containing some of his ashes that I wear when I feel the need to. At first, I wore it constantly. Over time, I wear it less and less. In my mind, that is progress in my journey toward peace. Colton is not in the necklace.

Chapter 12

My Rock

I have seen marriages fall apart because of child loss. There are varying articles online, but the average is 16%. One spouse just cannot handle the changes in the other. Their world has crumbled, and their dreams have shattered. They have no clue how to comfort each other, or themselves. They may blame one another. Yet, somehow life keeps chugging along like nothing happened, like the one you love most in the world has not died and left you broken. The bills still need to be paid; chores need to be done. The day-to-day responsibilities do not simply take care of themselves. You lived through the initial shock of death. Now, you must begin to deal with life. If you ever needed your mate this would be the time.

My husband has been nothing short of amazing during this entire journey of loss with me. He was an amazing stepdad to Colton for the 10 years that he knew him. He has been there for me with 100% non-judgmental support since Colton passed. During the 6 weeks that I was staying in Prince George with Colton, Randy had to drive back and forth several times to Alberta for work and to look after our lives there. I never heard one negative thing come out of his mouth for the hardship that he was enduring. He felt bad leaving me, worrying constantly about everything but knowing that I was well cared for staying with Barb and Dave and that I was where I needed to be.

I am sure he wondered how different I would be "afterwards." I mean, he certainly did not sign up for this! (Unless you believe that we all choose our journey before we are born based on the lessons that we feel we need to learn and the things that we would like to experience, but that is a different chapter, even a different book.)

I have relied heavily on my husband for support. There were lots of days where we just existed together, curled up with snacks watching television. He would cook when I was unable to get up. He would never let me see how much he must have been grieving also. He has shown me the kind of love that from the core of my being I never thought I would ever experience. He held me when I could not carry my own weight. He has listened to me sob my heart out on countless occasions, often saying "it is ok to cry," or "I know, it just hits you." He has never made me feel anything except supported and loved, and for that I am eternally grateful.

Being a bereaved parent is the hardest thing that life can throw at you. It is the curveball of all curveballs. The last thing I would wish on anyone is to do it all alone. Do not get me wrong, there are plenty of times that I feel alone. A part of me is now missing. But it is the strength that I get from knowing that Randy is here with me to help me along on this journey toward peace that makes me think that I can survive this...even thrive.

We found comfort in each other. We found that together is far better than apart could ever be. We are closer now in many ways as we weather this storm together than we have ever been. Our future looks different now than before Colton left. I had to re-read that last line, then stop, and think. I never thought there would ever be plans made that did not include my son, yet here we are.

If you are reading this and you are a bereaved mother, I hope you have a Randy in your life.

If you are my Randy and you are reading this, I love you more than you will ever know, and thank you for being my stronghold, my rock.

Chapter 13

Grief Settles In

Now that Colton's Celebration of Life was over, we got ready to go back to Cochrane. On our last day in Prince George, I was able to ensure that Colton's ashes were picked up and would safely come home with me. The loose ends were tied up. Goodbyes and Thank Yous were said, the trailer packed and hooked up and ready to go. It was so extremely hard to say goodbye to Barb. I had an idea of how much I would need her support in the coming weeks and months as I tried to find my new "normal." (Spoiler alert, there is no such thing...nothing normal about this ride, I assure you). I had no idea what to expect once I was home and Randy was at work, and I was truly alone for the first time. I knew that I was not the kind of person to reach out. I keep to myself.

The trip over the Rockies was beautiful, treacherous, and seemed to take forever, but we made it home safely. Our dog Louie was so happy to be back in his yard! There were a couple of things that did not go well, but in hindsight, because of the time of year they were bound to happen. There had been a power outage and, while brief, it knocked the power off to the hot tub and the pump froze and was destroyed. We found that taking the trailer on those long trips in the middle of winter rusted and seized the brakes, things like that. They seemed like huge things at the time, because we were both stretched so thin that we simply could not take one single thing on top of what we were already carrying.

I remember it being bitterly cold. Of course, it was January in Cochrane Alberta. I was numb. We both were. I know that Randy was happy that we were home and that he could look after me, look after the house, and look after his store. His team was extremely supportive of us both, and I am so thankful for that. It is true, most people do not know what to say to you after a tremendous loss such as mine. There is nothing. That is why they say, "I am so sorry for your loss." That is fine. I remember that it was the ones that said nothing that hurt me the most. They know who they are, and they must live with that. I remember not wanting to leave the house. I just wanted comfort. There were many boxes of wine that were to be sacrificed in the weeks, months, even years ahead. I just wanted to be numb. I did not know how to begin to unravel everything that had happened. In hindsight, was this a wise decision? Oh, hell no, but I simply did not care. There were many comfort dishes of cheesy pasta, hearty stews, and lots of snacks. There was just this icy cold place that started in my head, circled my heart, and landed in the pit of my stomach. Nothing can fill the hole of loss.

One thing that Randy and I did was a little retail therapy. Shortly after we got home, we went to Costco and bought 2 65-inch TVs. One went over the fireplace in our living room and the other created a cozy retreat downstairs. We put our 2 loveseats together in a square and filled it with blankets and pillows. We called it our 'nest.' There were quite a few days that I did not leave the nest. I binge watched everything I could find on YouTube about grief, about what happens when you die, about near-death experiences. I watched shows about life after death, reincarnation, psychic mediums, and whatever else I could find.

And I cried. I wailed. I rocked back and forth calling his name aloud. Hours and hours and days and days on end. I exhausted myself so that I could get some sleep.

Somedays I could drag myself around like a zombie, crying and cooking, crying and laundry.

When I had the strength to go out, crying and shopping. Randy did much of the cooking during these first few weeks. I remember one day; I drove about 30 minutes away to shop for a pair of glasses. I found the store, but when I went in and had a brief look around, I was approached by a salesperson and was overcome with such extreme anxiety that I choked out an apology, turned and left, got in my car, and drove straight to Randy's store and walked straight into his arms. I have never felt so helpless or unable to cope in my entire life. At night, I would cry and cry until I could not breathe, sometimes causing Randy great anxiety as well. There was nothing he could do except hold me and let me cry. As I think back to that time, the tears flow all over again. It was the beginning of the lowest part of my life.

Chapter 14

Dreams

Shortly after we returned home after Colton's Celebration of Life, a month and a half or so, he came to me for his first visit. He was sitting on the edge of the bed looking at me. He was wearing a red T-shirt. He was smiling a beautiful happy smile. He looked younger than 26, closer to 19 or 20. He said, "I'm here now." I said, "In heaven?" He did not answer, but he leaned toward me, so I leaned toward him, and he said, "You smell good, I've missed that smell." Then he was gone. Of course, I am sobbing as I type this because it was SO REAL. I can still see every detail of that moment. I do believe that it was a visit, not a dream, as it was not something I would have expected him to say. It felt true to me.

Sometimes I would hear him calling me. One night this happened, and I could faintly hear him, then it got louder and louder. He finally reached me, and I heard his voice yell "Mom!" and without thinking I sat up in bed and yelled "What?!" before I realized that it was in my head. I truly felt like I was losing my mind.

On one occasion I had gone to bed early with a pressure headache. I had been working outside all day, so I thought I got too much sun or was a bit dehydrated. I could not sleep but that was nothing new. Those who are grieving often cannot sleep, or have trouble falling asleep, as our minds are full of memories and painful images that run on a loop. I drank 2 ½ liters of water throughout the night, trying to alleviate the headache, which of course meant getting up to pee. After getting up at 3:15am I did not think I would fall back asleep, but then I had a visit from Colton. He was much younger, 17 or 18. The details of the dream are weird and made no sense, so I will not type them out. The highlight of the dream for me was a hug. I got one. The rest was sad, resigned and ended confusingly. I woke up with a huge gasp as I could not catch my breath, and then the tears which woke Randy up concerned and upset. Then his alarm went off, and that was how the day started. It made me think this: "What the hell, I was doing so well lately. Several good, happier days in a row, and now this?" Then I thought, I will not let it consume me today. Yeah, sure. Grief is unpredictable.

Colton does not visit that often in my dreams, and I often wish that he would. I have come to understand that the better frame of mind that I am in, the greater the likelihood that it will happen. So, it made sense that it happened after I had a few good days.

As the first Christmas without him approached, he came to me in a dream to tell me what to get for his girlfriend as a gift. He made a motion with his hands like something was very thin, and then I saw the leather bracelet on his wrist (they wore matching ones for a while). Then he gave me a little side hug and said, "I've got to go now momma," and it was over. The next day I told Randy about the dream and how I had seen bracelets in a shop downtown that I thought might be what he was talking about. So, we went to check it out. We walked into the little gift shop and there was a tray of several different kinds. As I picked one up, I said, "I wonder if this is what he meant?" As I read the engraving I had to laugh because in all one word it read, "absofuckinglutely," so I bought it and that was that. Later when I gave it to her and told her of the dream, she said, "that sounds like him."

There have only been a handful of visits from Colton. When it happens, I remember each, and every detail and they stay with me. It is not like a regular dream that you forget by the time you have had your breakfast. One time, it was just a young, sweet version of him that was so happy and just wanted a hug from me, his arms wide open. He had bleached hair so that told me that he was 10 or 12 years old. There were no words, just a big smile and a tight warm hug. I say warm because I could feel it. And then it was over. Then I wake up and I cry, and cry and it is hard to breathe, and it takes a long time to recover. I would not trade those visits for the world, but, man oh man, they are hard on the heart.

Sometimes I feel like he is doing his best to get through to me. In hospice, I gave him permission to haunt me, and we smiled at each other. He just said, "I will see what I can do, Mom. "I feel like I try to get through to him every single day. But really, it is just that there is so much that I want to say to him or show him that I just talk to him. Aloud. I mean, why not? You never know, he could be right there beside me. There have been many occasions when our dog will sit at attention and stare at the corner of the room. I get up and look but there is nothing there. Or, he has stopped by to hang out for a while. It got to the point that when that happens now, I just say, "Hi honey."

I remember years and years ago after Randy and I bought our first house together in Prince George, Colton told me that when we were not home, sometimes he liked to lay on our bed because it was so comfortable and watch TV or use the computer. I told him that was weird but ok and never thought much about it. After he passed, one of his friends sent me a YouTube video of him and Colton dancing around like wackos in our bedroom because that is where the computer was, and they were goofing around online. Of course, it was painful and comforting at the same time. In fact, there are a collection of silly videos that I can watch if I need to. Finding them later was like finding lost treasure, and I watched them repeatedly. Less so, now, but it is comforting to know they are there if I need them. Then, in Alberta, Randy and I would be watching TV downstairs in our nest, and we would hear someone get off our bed and walk across the floor. We would just look at each other and say, "you heard that, right?" I believe he is still around. That sweet loving energy is with me. It brings me comfort and rips my heart out at the same time. I am sure that every bereaved parent would agree with me.

Chapter 15

Grief, and Gratitude?

Definition: a feeling of thankfulness, appreciation. Next poses the question: What the hell does gratitude have to do with losing my son? Am I to be grateful for the experience of watching him get Cancer and die before my eyes? Well, no, not initially. But, in the long term, after what seems to be an eternity of sleepless nights, heart-wrenching pain, panic, anxiety...yes. Even after crying an ocean of tears? Yes. Can Gratitude and Grief sit in the same chair together? Even get along? Yes.

I feel like I waited a long time for Colton. When he arrived, I believed there was nothing more beautiful than this amazing child in my arms. That full head of dark hair and those gorgeous blue eyes! At 26, I was nervous but ready to raise the best little man that I could. He was never a problem, always such a joy to have with me. He grounded me, made me a better person than I would have been without him, without a doubt. Yes, it was a challenge. He was never quite in perfect health. Always a runny nose like a new puppy, or a fever. I was stuck trying to find out why, and there were many, many trips to the Dr.'s office or the ER when he was little. But we always persevered, the two of us. When Colton was 3, I tried to give him a brother or sister, but it was not to be, and I miscarried in the fourth month. At that moment, I knew that it was going to be just Colton and I against the world, but we had each other.

I did my best to instill in him the skills and lessons that he would need to be a happy and independent man, and he was. We had the love and the close-knit bond that I wanted and that I am profoundly grateful for. If there was something he wanted to tell me, he did. No matter how embarrassing or personal the questions were, I answered them as a mother, sometimes as a father, always with love and always with logic and truth. We had mutual trust.

It is a helpless feeling when your child gets sick. After exhausting everything that you have in your skill set, you are left with leaving it up to the professionals. Then, you have nothing to offer but love and support. But aren't those things of the greatest importance anyway?

Was I a good mother? What a loaded question to ask yourself! Of course, in hindsight, there are things that I would have handled differently. Lots of things.

But I would not have changed the relationship we had for anything, because nothing compares to it. I was told by so many of his friends that I was his favorite person, and of course there were lots of "love you momma" moments for me to treasure, but I still have my doubts. Did I do everything in my power to save him? I believe so. It is a tough pill to swallow that I will never know for sure.

I am grateful that there are so many memories of times that we shared. Movie nights with huge bowls of buttered popcorn, family dinners (he was such a meat and potatoes boy!) and lots of times that he was there for me. He was my 'pilot car' on the 10-hour drive to say goodbye to my father before he passed. Even at his age, he was wise and always had a well thought out opinion when asked for it, and he gave it with maturity, logic, and tact beyond his years. As if it is not obvious here, I am an extremely proud mother.

Oddly enough, the internet has been useful in my search for gratitude and in understanding the grieving process. Grief is a powerful emotion, equal to love, and has tremendous effects on us, our relationships, our families, our health, and our communities. It is important. And it gets ignored.

Over time, I have learned a lot about my own grief and how I react to it. I have also learned, for better or worse, how others react to it. There is a stigma attached to it. Awe, she is the one who lost her only child, poor, pitiful thing! Although it is universal, each person's grief experience is unique. No one can make your journey for you, and no one is qualified to give you your own personal set of directions for the trip.

So, a long time later, I can see my grief from a unique perspective, with Gratitude. I am so thankful that I had the opportunity to know this sweet hearted, kind, and generous person, my son. I have learned more than I thought I would ever need to know about a great many horrible things. I also learned more than I thought I would ever need to know about a great many wonderful things. And, if knowledge is power, then just maybe, that makes me a little bit stronger.

Thank you, Colton, for being mine. I am so grateful that you are.

Chapter 16

Back to Work

So, I made a huge mistake. A couple of weeks after our return to Alberta, I was bawling my eyes out and staring out at the snow, when my phone rang. I did not recognize the number but, like an idiot, I picked it up anyway. It was my Regional Manager checking in to see how I was doing. That was a lovely gesture, however he also asked when I was coming back to work. I had not thought about that yet. Or, I had thought about it and knew I did not want to. He had a couple of options for me. One was to go back to the store I was working in before Colton's passing and one was to go to a completely different store. I chose to go back to where I knew people would hopefully understand what I had just been through. And so, after only 4 weeks, I returned to work. Let me be honest here, I was not ready. I remember thinking that it might be good for me to stay busy, Also, I had recently watched a Ted Talk on YouTube about grief, and the woman said that you cannot stay on your couch forever with that glass of wine and bowl of pasta. And I was literally sitting on my couch with a glass of wine and a bowl of pasta! I remember Randy and I looking at each other like, wow, did she just say that?

This began an exceedingly challenging time in my grief journey. My shifts were not consistent, so sometimes I had to get up early to prepare myself mentally and physically for the 1-hour drive, followed by the 9 or 10-hour shift, then the 1-hour drive home. Other times I had to close the store so I would grieve all morning, then be gone all afternoon and evening, not see Randy at all, and get in just before midnight. Sometimes a closing shift was followed by an early shift. While at the store, there were lots of details to distract me, but quite often they did not work. There were many times I would be overcome by grief. More than once I took over my Store Managers' office and called Barb to cry and talk. There were entire stretches of time that I simply do not remember. Mostly, I avoided everyone, kept my head down and did my job. I would get home exhausted, but unable to sleep. One night, I remember getting home at 11:45pm, and pouring a glass of wine (as usual). I was grieving hard all the way home. I had pulled out my deck of angel cards. I focused and asked for a message from Colton. Only Light. Only Truth. I shuffled that deck like you would not believe. I asked, "Where are you?" I waited a moment and turned over the card I had chosen. It read, "I'm standing right beside you." I will never forget that as long as I live. It was a total goosebump moment, and I cried my eyes out. It was experiences like this that kept me going through this dark time.

There were a few coworkers that helped me. One, Caroline, was my angel during that time. She knew when I was having a rough day and would suddenly need me out in the vestibule entrance area to ask me a question, but really, she just knew that I needed to talk or cry, or both. She gifted me with a lovely solar angel garden light that reads "Beyond the darkness, Light. Beyond the sorrow, Peace." Of course, I burst into tears when she gave it to me. One night, years later, I was sitting on my deck and asking Colton for a sign, and at that exact moment, the little lantern lit up.

It took a long time to get back into work mode. The career that I had worked so many years to achieve, things that I had wanted so badly had suddenly lost their meaning. Climbing that corporate ladder just began to seem unimportant. Grief was changing my priorities. I thought, "without Colton, what is the point of all this?"

Chapter 17

A Leap of Faith

Not long after we were back in Alberta, we went to Campbell River to visit Randy's family and look at properties for sale. We had a realtor take us to view a few houses and gave her our criteria. I told her my story and told her that I needed to be able to see the ocean, to heal my soul. We needed enough space for our dog and RV parking. That was it. She showed us a place that we fell in love with, and we made an offer, well above the asking price. We even wrote a letter explaining our story and how much it would mean to us; however, the seller chose an offer with no conditions. I cried when we lost it.

We spent time at the lake property whenever we went to the island. Mostly, I just feel joy being there. It gave me a taste of how I will live out the rest of my days and even find a little peace and calm in this second half of my journey. I remember reading one of those posts about grieving and it stuck...that there are only two times: the time before you died and the time since. There is only "life before" and "life after."

We were on day 7 here at the off-grid cabin, and some of the dead trees were taken down and cut to length for firewood but needed to be split. There is an electric log splitter that, when attached to the generator, makes this job easy. As I was running the splitter I was overcome with emotion and was sobbing uncontrollably because I was remembering the Christmas that Colton had purchased this for us. This huge box was under the tree, and he was immensely proud of it. Randy and I were stunned to see what it was and touched that he would think of this. He said, "this is to make it easier to be at the cabin when you're old and can't split wood anymore." We laughed at the time and thanked him for thinking of us, but seeing how he was thinking ahead for us was an emotional trigger for me, and out came the grief in a waterfall of tears. As Randy saw that I was having a meltdown, I tried to put into words what I was remembering, I could see the memory on his face as well. It was a realization that this gift from years ago was coming true and was making this job a whole lot easier. Colton was never able to come out to the cabin and see this beautiful place, yet I know he was right there beside me, seeing how easy it was to split the wood.

Here, without the distraction of cell phones, the internet, and the demands of regular life, I can think. I can clear my mind. Sometimes that lack of distraction results in hardcore grieving, like this memory that hit me upside the head like a baseball bat, but it seems to be the good, cleansing kind. Usually, I can think and remember and be ok with whatever I remember, sometimes with tears of gratitude and sometimes with no tears for a change. Sitting around the campfire at night with my husband, his two sisters and their husbands and having a few drinks, I often feel a tiny bit stronger. Like I can find a group here that will help me navigate my way through this. The good, creative, happy days and the days that are dark and heavy and oh so extremely hard to carry. It was a great vacation, but soon we had to head back to Alberta.

Not long after we were home, our realtor gave us a call, and told us of a house that was not on the market. She knew the couple; they were elderly and wanting to downsize. They were thinking of moving to Kelowna where their son lived. She thought the place would be perfect for us. So, Randy's sister did a video walk through with her cell phone, I saw the ocean, and that was it. We relied on family and made the choice to buy our retirement home. Let it be said that we were not retired. Also, we already had a house in Cochrane. Also, there was not even a transfer on the horizon for us! This was nuts! But here is the thing: I had lost my fear. Before Colton left, I was always so worried about money, about the future, about work. Now, I knew that the absolute worst thing that could ever happen to me had already happened. So, I said yes, let's do it. We got the house, thanks to a realtor that cared about what we needed, the divine timing of my parents' estate being settled and my portion being enough to cover the downpayment...

As there is a tremendous shortage of housing in Campbell River, we had many applications of renters to sort through, and in the end, relied heavily on Randy's parents to meet and screen potential applicants. It took a while, but the previous owners decided to stay on for a couple of months to get their plans in place to move so it worked out fine for us. I still scratch my head and wonder how we managed to juggle 2 mortgages, be landlords, work and grieve all at the same time. It was a whirlwind that lasted until something even crazier happened.

Chapter 18

A Promotion and a Pandemic

I was given the opportunity to be promoted to Assistant Store Manager and, at the same time, to open a new store from start to finish. This is an enormous undertaking at the best of times. I was to be working with a young Store Manager, just a few years older than Colton was. During my interview for the job, I told her that I was grieving the recent loss of my son as I felt that she should be aware that there were going to be days when my grief would affect me. As it turned out we could not have had more different management styles. This proved to be a challenge in many ways. The lack of empathy I received from her was shocking at times. She was all business, and simply could not relate to my situation at all, whereas I was becoming all about the team members. This was a change for me as I was once very driven regarding my career. I learned a great deal in this new role. Not only about the business of running a store but also how losing Colton was changing me as a person, as well as a leader. I was far more approachable. I cared more about the people on my team, and in turn, I felt the team rally around me. During this time, I learned more about grief. I learned that because I was still wearing my grief all over my face, I became a magnet for every team member who had suffered a loss. They knew that because I survived the ultimate loss, the unthinkable one, that I would listen and understand as they shared their stories with me. There were days when my grief was raw and ripped wide open. But now, I had found a source of comfort with those who now knew that it was ok to not be ok. It felt like a tiny step forward.

It was coming up to the first Christmas without Colton. Since we had moved to Alberta, we had spent the last 2 Christmases just the two of us because, when you are both managers in grocery stores, it is all but impossible to take vacation during the holidays. Also, travelling over the Rockies in the middle of winter is not ideal, as we had found out during his illness. This year, for some reason, Randy was having a Griswold moment and had decided to put up a ton of Christmas lights and decorations. He brought the tree and ornaments upstairs and said "go on, put it up. It will do you some good." I thought Oh Hell No, but before I could argue with him, he was back outside hanging more lights. And so, while crying into my wine and remembering Christmases past, I put up the tree. Yes, it did me some good. What did I think I would do, sit in the dark through the holiday season? Well, yes actually, I was prepared for that. I was not prepared for what was coming next.

At work the week before Christmas, it was extremely busy at the store, and I was running around like mad when I got a text from Randy. There was no message, just a picture of a Shih Tzu puppy. It was adorable, but my text back was a short "Nope!" Later, he told me that a man had walked into his store with this pup under his arm and told Randy that he and his wife had driven from Manitoba to visit for the holidays. This was the last pup of the litter. The person who was to pick her up had suddenly passed away and they had no choice but to bring her along. Randy asked if she was for sale, and of course she was. He got the address of where they were staying, and when I got home, I was convinced to "just go and see her." Right. So, that was how Randy bought our dog Daisy at the grocery store. All he had to say was that he thought that I needed another heartbeat to look after, and that maybe Colton sent her to us. I was a goner. I mean, how was I supposed to say no after that speech? Louie was less than impressed by this new addition. With that, we added puppy training to our busy schedule, and she became a member of the family.

During the entire year of 2019, I continued my spiritual journey, looking for answers to all the questions that burned in my mind. I read books written by different mediums, taking comfort in the stories of others that had experienced great loss, and yet somehow, were finding their path to peace, and some having incredible messages from their loved ones who had passed. This subject fascinated me.

On days off with Randy, we would take our pups to a beautiful off leash dog park along the Bow River near our house. While they ran around and played with all the dogs, Randy and I had a chance to walk and talk about our day and about our desire to move to Campbell River. In our jobs, we would have to wait until a position became available, so moving from an area that was growing so fast to a retirement town with only 1 store was indeed a long shot at best. But our desire never diminished, and we continued to focus on it. In our minds, the decision had already been made.

Every time we were able to take a vacation, we drove to the island and checked on our house there. Renting it was not ideal, we knew there would be damage to repair. Some changes and updates had to be made before the renters moved in, and there was always something we were able to accomplish while we were there. Just standing on the deck and looking at the ocean was like a salve for my soul. I longed for the day when we could finally move in. When our tenants' first year lease was up, we only renewed it for another 6 months and let her know that we had made plans to move in (even though we had no job offer, nothing was written in stone, and we were acting completely on intuition.)

Slowly, against all logic it seemed, we began to prepare for our move to Vancouver Island. We completely landscaped our yard in Cochrane. We built a retaining wall and fence. We painted the entire main floor of the house. To say we kept busy was an enormous understatement. It helped me at the time; however, I knew that I was not taking the time I needed to properly grieve. In the conversations that I had with Barb during that time, she mentioned that I should investigate seeing a grief counselor. I understood that she was worried about me. I was worried about me too. I was angry. I was exhausted. But what I told her then is how I still feel that unless the counselor was a mother who had lost her only son then she could not understand what I was going through. Now, I know that they are trained to share the coping strategies that they have learned in school, and I am sure that I could have benefited in some way. It seems that throughout my life, if there was a harder way to do something, I would find it. My grief journey would prove to be no different.

Every fall, our company honors those who have reached a milestone year of service. Loyalty points are given to those with 5, 10, 15 etc. years of service. My 25th year, and Randy's 35th year had the 2 of us receiving a considerable number of points, which can be used for travel. With our points we planned to take Barb and Dave on a trip with us to Cancun Mexico, to thank them for their support during the absolute worst time in my life. Of course, they excitedly accepted. Just before we left for the trip, Barb and I were finding little white feathers. She even found one in her suitcase! We had gone to walk the dogs down by the river, and we saw the most beautiful white fluffy dog with bright blue eyes. Barb asked the young man what the dog's name was, and it was Colton's last name. We just looked at each other and shook our heads, as clearly, this trip was a great idea. At least, Colton thought so because there was our sign! We relaxed on the beach, we took a bus tour of Chichen Itza, the Mexican ruins on the Yucatan peninsula. We visited Isla Mujeres and rented a golf cart to tour the island. It was a trip to remember, and I am grateful that we could make it happen.

Before I knew it, the end of the second year was fast approaching. I was doing whatever I could to cope. I was keeping up at work, keeping up at home, and trying to make plans to move...grieving all the way.

Anything can trigger your feelings of loss. A photograph, the lyrics of a song, a certain smell, a date on the calendar, seeing a product on a shelf in the grocery store. It can make a very private thing turn into a public spectacle.

Heading into the first Christmas season after Colton died, I was on the job. During this time of year, the store is inundated with countless pallets of merchandise that come on little cardboard display stands known as shippers. The goal is to build and put these out in strategic locations as quickly as possible to capture sales as customers are shopping spontaneously for the Christmas season. Most of them are chocolate. Some of them only come in at Christmas time, and shoppers rush to get their families' favorites before they sell out.

Colton had his favorite too, Terry's Chocolate Oranges. Every single year, without fail, I would buy one for his stocking. So, there I was on my hands and knees building a Christmas display when I got to the shipper of his favorites. In a split second I froze. The familiar lump formed in my throat, and my breathing felt constricted. The tears burned and began to roll down my face. The now-familiar pain racked my body and I started to panic. I remember almost stepping back from myself, and thinking "Whoa, get it together girl, it is just a shipper of chocolate ", but it was far too late for that. So, I loaded a deck with cardboard and made a hasty exit into the warehouse where I only had one or two team members to deal with rather than a hoard of Christmas shoppers. I remember the sad looks, the kind words of compassion from those that understood grief. I remember calling Randy to tell him what happened and hearing his encouraging words. Finally, after a few minutes I was able to acknowledge the intensity of the trigger and move on with my workday. It strikes me as hard today as it did back then to relive that moment. To relive any moment that drives home the fact that Colton will not be here to enjoy it again. Then, shortly after that day, I was looking through the weekly flyer bundle that comes in the paper. A simple thing. But, once again, it was a trigger.

Colton's favorite pie, lemon merengue was on sale. The familiar lump in the throat, the shortness of breath, the tears. Over a picture of pie! My reaction made me think: Is this the case for all the bereaved mothers out there? I posted the question to a Facebook grief group that I was a part of. I could not believe the response! My messages were flooded by over a hundred mothers who happened to see my experience and feel it as their own. Comments came from all over the world about how they have not been able to set foot in a grocery store since their son died for fear of seeing his favorite cereal, his favorite frozen pizza...whatever it was. I spent the next couple of days responding to these mothers, if only to let them know that they are not alone, they are not crazy, they are grieving. When I can, I try to lift their spirits a little, in hopes of lifting my own. I had a brief but funny comment or two with a mom whose son worked in a grocery store and had wanted to teach her turkey bowling...! She thanked me for her chance to smile at the memory. To me, that is such a valuable thing now. Many days come and go, and I can look at his pictures and smile, and the memories warm my heart, even if they are accompanied by sadness and grief. Still, there are days when I avoid looking because I am too close to the edge of my grief. I am sure that this feeling is universal in the world of the bereaved mother, but even if it is not, it is mine to deal with. When I am overcome with emotion, I write about it. Yes, it is painful, and yes, I cry a LOT when I do it (as I am now). Still, there is more room out than in, and at least for me, I feel better when it is out. Sometimes I feel like I am just making room for more grief but that is ok too. This is not going away and will continue until my last grateful breath. And if someone who is grieving reads this and feels a connection to it, a camaraderie if you will, then it is worth it to me. On one hand, I write to leave a lasting account of this grief journey and to immortalize my memories of Colton, the ways my life has changed since his passing, and as a way of dealing with feelings that are sometimes too big and too difficult to share on any given day. It helps me keep him present. But also, I do it so that there is a chance that I will reach someone who is hurting the same way that I am, and that by reading it they gain a better understanding that what they are going through can be managed, can be nurtured, can be cathartic. There will be triggers. They are everywhere. The time of day, a photo, the season, a birthday, the date of your loved ones' passing. Images, sounds, and smells that bring us to a long-lost moment in time. They cannot be avoided, but recognized, acknowledged, held for a moment in remembrance, then let go... Like their favorite Christmas chocolate or a piece of pie. When I was going through journals in preparation for this book, I found an entry from January 29, 2020. It was a difficult day. Rather than paraphrase it, I will include it in its' entirety. Re-reading it now, it is such an accurate description of what many days were like for me at that time:

January 29, 2020. Grief is exhausting. Some days it feels like you have been picked up and thrown against a brick wall. Yesterday was one of those days for me. It was my day off and I had grand plans of being productive. Instead, I felt heavy and dark. Unable to leave the house. Usually when I feel this way I make coffee, check Facebook for an uplifting post or to check in and see what people I know are doing, then go on YouTube and find a video or two that I feel a connection with about the other side and how our loved ones are with us. Sometimes this works for me and then I can go on with my day, get my chores done. It did not work, though. I had such tightness in my chest. I thought it was anxiety. I thought I was having a heart attack, or I was getting a chest infection. What a debilitating feeling! It was simply grief. Simply, complicated grief. I know this because random things on TV or Netflix would make me cry. Really cry. Like crying so hard that you are glad for a moment that you are alone. At one point I did not want to be alone at all, but I was and the only person I have is Randy. He knew I was having an unbelievably difficult day because we stayed connected by phone all the time. He came home for lunch to check on me and I was just curled up in the 'nest.' We do not have people over. It is just us. He told me it is ok to have a lazy day if I do not feel good. He knows what to say to me. He is my only person now. Grief is lonely. As often as my friend or my sister checks in, once a month or so, it cannot compare to the nonstop barrage of thought, memory, and absolute pain of heartache that occurs daily. I mentioned this last memory to Randy. He reminded me that our neighbors in Cochrane did invite us over on a couple of occasions. I do remember saying no, I just could not bring myself to be social. It was too painful. He did not push me to be ready, and I am grateful for that. I should have pushed myself. Grief blocked me. I did not want to fake being ok, but in hindsight, it would have done me a world of good. Grief sucks. Thankfully, as more time passed, Randy formed a friendship with a coworker and her spouse, and as I got to know them, I knew we were meant to meet. She had lost her husband and he had lost his wife to cancer. They understood grief. I did not have to fake anything; they knew where I was on my journey. I was to learn this time after time: if you can keep the door to your heart open, even just a crack, you will find your people. You will never let them go.

After Randy went back to work, I watched a couple of episodes of a show that he liked and found helpful with his grief. It was. So, I got up and went upstairs to continue sorting through all the paperwork in the office. This is the last room that needs to be organized before we get ready to sell the house. The beautiful blue trunk that I bought to put Colton's things in is full and sitting on top of Daisy's doghouse that I am in the middle of painting. Projects everywhere. The trunk is full, but I have not sorted through it. I need to organize his papers, take pictures and documents out of frames and into protectors and get it all sorted. I know this task must be done in tiny bits. It is far too painful, and any tiny bit can be the end of the day for me. A picture. His old passport. Anything. So, I lift the trunk to take it into the spare bedroom. It is heavy. I struggle. I started crying. I managed to get it where I wanted it and went back to try and get some work done. Instead, I fell to my knees and started screaming. Wailing. Making noises that only one who has lost a piece of their soul could make. I was so loud I was certain that the neighbors could hear me. After a while I got up and blew my nose and cleaned myself up a bit. But now I knew that I was not having a heart attack. It was anxiety. It was a grieving day. Simple yet so complicated that it took the entire day for me to figure it out. I was physically and emotionally exhausted and just hung out in my house for the entire day. And that is ok. I thanked my husband for his understanding and apologized for being so broken. Brokenhearted. He said, "We are all a bit broken, right?"

Today is also a day off. I woke up just before 10am. I usually wake up early. I am still exhausted. It is a better day. I feel like I will be able to get some laundry done, gas up the car, get ready for the next work week. Doing this work of writing is so beneficial. Each time that I write about my grief journey I know I am taking a tiny step in the right direction and that one day, this journal will help another mom (or dad) like me. One takeaway from yesterday. Now that I feel a bit stronger today, I think that if someone close to me loses a child, I will be able to recognize that they will need more. More care. More calls and texts. Especially if they do not have a network of people around them that they love and trust. Somedays, I understand that they will need to be alone. A simple daily text will do. Do not expect that they will respond. If they do, it may be a word or two, and that is fine. But the text will be read and appreciated, and the griever will feel less alone for a moment. Grief is exhausting. It is the same size as love.

In February, every year all the Store Managers gather in Langley B.C. for convention. This is a time for them to hear news about the company and where it is headed, financial reports, team building motivational speakers rally the group, and plans are made for the upcoming year as they break out into groups by region. They are fed and entertained, and hopefully come back rejuvenated. At the end of the convention, a yearbook of sorts is handed out, with pictures of all the VPs and of all the Store Managers. My reason for including this is this: When Randy got home from his convention, I had picked up the book and was looking at the 'mug shots' of all the Store Managers to see who I recognized. The Campbell River store did not have a picture of its' Store Manager. Shortly after, a temporary position was posted! Randy and I briefly weighed the pros and cons of him applying for this, but we knew one thing; this was our opportunity! I just knew, I could feel it in my bones, that this would turn into a permanent posting and that Randy would be chosen. He called his regional manager to let him know that that is where we wanted to go. He was already aware of our desire to move there, and that we had a house to go to. So, Randy put in for the move.

Then, it was March of 2020. News about a new virus that was spreading around the globe was making headlines. Travel was compromised. On the day that international travel was restricted, my Store Manager had flown to Mexico on vacation. Then all hell broke loose.

Unfortunately, she had the Store Manager's phone with her. As Health protocols were changing several times a day, I had to rely on texts and calls from Randy as he received the information. Things like "quick, get on the computer, there's another conference call!"

It was truly a surreal time to be on the front lines as an essential worker. As well as healthcare, grocery stores, liquor stores, gas stations and the like remained open. With restaurants closed, people bought groceries and cooked at home like never before. Remember when everyone started making their own bread? The stores ran out of yeast! We knew from the first few days that something big was going on as certain groups would come in and buy shopping carts filled to overflowing with hand sanitizer, gloves, masks, disinfectant wipes, toilet paper and paper towels. It was so unusual. Shoppers were fearful. They were demanding and rude. Our suppliers could not keep up with the demand, resulting in empty shelves. I had never witnessed panic buying prior to this and it made me uneasy. The days grew longer. 12-to-14-hour days were the norm. Suddenly, we all had to wear masks, and gloves, and hire people whose sole purpose was to routinely clean all touchable surfaces every few hours! Many of our team members were fearful and stayed home. Some were immunocompromised and had to stay home. Some did get sick, resulting in heaps of paperwork, recording of dates and times and when and what department they worked in, who they were in contact with, all of it.

As the fear intensified, there I was working on the front lines, a brand-new Assistant now thrust into the role of acting Store Manager. Health protocols were changing several times a day, customers were hoarding dry goods and I had been told where to go and how to get there by more than one angry customer. It was the most stressful of times.

One night during this time, Colton came to me in a dream. In the dream someone came up to me in the store and said, "your son is outside crying." I ran outside and he was sitting in a car in the parking lot. When he saw me, he got out and we hugged. He said, "Mom, I'm so sorry you have to work during the pandemic." I said, "will I get Covid?" He said, "no, I am protecting you," Then he was gone. In the dream, some of the people could see him and some could not. It was a great feeling of comfort for me at the time. I also happen to believe that he was protecting me, and from that moment, although I followed all the protocols anyway, I never feared that I would get the virus, and I never did.

There was a world of stress that rested on my inexperienced shoulders during that time. I made a lot of phone calls and asked a lot of questions. The regional manager was calling or texting throughout that time to ensure that everything was running as smoothly as possible. But here is what happened...

The entire team supported me! By this time, there was not a single department manager that complained about not having the Store Manager there and were more than happy to come to work and deal with the absolute craziness of what was happening to all of us daily. I am sure that I got a few things wrong, but I did my absolute best in a very uncertain time. No one seemed to notice. We rolled with the changes. We lightened the mood when we were yelled at and sometimes cursed at by the panicky customers. The store was run, the reports were entered, stock was ordered and worked to the shelf. Policies and procedures were executed. Things changed on a daily, sometimes hourly basis.

I remember the regional manager sitting with me one day, asking me, "Are you sure you don't want to be a Store Manager?" I said "Yes, I am sure. A couple of years ago, I sure did. But losing Colton changed all that. He changed my priorities." He understood because he understood grief. Not everyone does. I was grateful that he found me competent, capable of doing the job. Grief changes everything. And sometimes, the stars align, and circumstances take a turn for the unbelievable.

Chapter 19

Journey to the Island

I remember seeing the announcement that Randy was to be the new Store Manager in Campbell River. We just looked at each other and honestly, words were not needed. Hugging and jumping up and down were needed! We manifested this! We knew what we wanted, needed, and acted accordingly. We took steps, crazy steps at times, (buying a 2nd house and packing to move!) but it worked! The next few months were a blur, the pandemic was in full blown panic mode, and we had a house to sell in a particularly challenging market.

By this time, I had a new Store Manager that I enjoyed working with and who was accepted quite enthusiastically by the entire team. She understood that it was my time to go, even though I did not have a job to go to. Truthfully, that fact did not bother me as much as it should have. I knew that the company would find something for me, and in the meantime, I had a house to paint and move into. I was sad to say goodbye to the friends I had gotten to know, the ones who accepted me and my story and had shared their stories with me. As someone on a grief journey, I know the importance of holding space for the ones of like mind that you find along the way. 2 things stand out for me about my last day there. One was the hug I received from my assistant Brenda (which she snuck as it was against the Covid 19 protocols), and the fact that I drove away with a smile on my face and a lighter feeling in my soul.

To try and save money, we decided to move ourselves rather than have the company move us. I am not sure this was less stressful in any way, but we managed to do it in 3 trips. 3 16-hour road trips including a 2-hour ferry ride, pulling a trailer full of our stuff. No small task indeed.

I had an idea. I wanted to wake up in my island house on my birthday at the end of July. Now, this idea was really pushing it, but Randy wanted to make it happen for me. I guess I could go into the horrors of packing our belongings into that trailer, but let me just say, neither one of us ever wants to do that again. We worked up until the last minute, said our goodbyes to our respective store teams. But also, we were both exhausted and anxious and flying by the seat of our pants, hoping that we could pull this off without a hitch. We still had not sold our house yet.

This would have to be done from a province away, which was not ideal.

It was the longest road trip ever. I was not comfortable driving the big truck pulling the heavy trailer, so Randy drove the entire way. We were exhausted and crabby, but we were home! I will tell you this: waking up in Campbell River on my birthday was the best gift I had received in years! Yes, everything was in chaos. Yes, everything needed to be patched and painted and all of that. But none of that mattered. I knew in my heart that we were now where we are meant to be. Now I could begin to heal.

I had time to reflect on the last 2 ½ years of my grieving process. I realized that being thrust back into the workforce less than 4 weeks after we got home from Colton's Celebration of Life really did a number on me in my attempts to grieve properly. I had no idea which end was up. I relied heavily on Randy while he was grieving too. I will be the first to say that there were many things that I should have done differently. Now, I would be given the chance to finally grieve. I had creative, productive work to do, but I also had time for some self-care. I could finally breathe.

So, while Randy got settled into his role at his new store, I got settled into making this old house a home for us, and on a personal level, some soul searching and self-evaluation.

As I began to work on gaining clarity and what made my heart and mind feel better, it felt like I needed to not simply focus on losing Colton, but it was also necessary to look at who I was before then as well. I think that once I started to really dig deep and examine what I thought about life and death, that was the beginning of the change that would take place in my life. Why did I believe so differently about things now that Colton had died?

It was important to do a review of the things I was taught as a child. I had done much of this when Colton was little and he and I were on our own, having left the organized religion of my youth. This religion had divided my family, causing tremendous heartbreak. Some of the fundamental teachings no longer rang true to me. I knew that Colton's energy was alive and well, only his body was gone. There are family members who will never see things the way I now know to be true. So, after much consideration, there was only one thing I could do:

forgive their absence during this time and try to let it go.

I know what you might be thinking. Seriously? They do not deserve that! Just hear me out: I discovered that not only did I need to give forgiveness to those who I felt wronged by during this life, but also to that rapidly aging face in my mirror. I had to let go of that heavy blanket of guilt, that there was something, anything, that I could have done differently to change this terrible outcome. I had to let go of the massive guilt that I felt for Colton's death. There is just something about being a mother. It is as if when they let you leave the hospital with your baby, someone says, "Oh hey, don't forget this," and hands you this huge bag of guilt that you must now carry around for the remainder of your days, because nothing you are about to do could possibly be good enough for this precious child. Could I have stopped Cancer from happening to my son? No. Does carrying around that feeling for the rest of my days serve me in any way? No. Am I now living in a state of divine self-forgiveness? Well, that is still a work in progress...

I believe that any self-improvement must begin with a massive cleanout of the residual cobwebs of utter crap that many of us were raised with. Erroneous beliefs and values from generations past. There are patterns of shame, self-doubt, and inadequacies that no longer ring true or serve us in any way. How does this relate to grief? At its core, grief is the mourning of a loss. So, losing a belief system, the approval of family members, the loss of failed, ill-chosen relationships, it all adds up to a nasty concoction of guilt saddled with grief. Ultimately, forgiving ourselves and others is an ongoing process. So is grief. Beginning this process puts us on the path toward peace.

Chapter 20

Self-care

So, now that we have moved in and live where we had wanted to be, everything is great, right? Nope! Somehow, my little black dust-ball of grief followed me here just like the little black dust-ball that followed Pigpen everywhere in the Peanuts' Comic Strip. (I thought you might like that visual.) Now, for the first time since those initial couple of weeks after Colton's Celebration of Life I was alone all day. Naturally, I spent a lot of time on my own thoughts. I now know that this was necessary in my grieving process, but it felt like I was taking huge steps backwards after the distraction of long workdays that kept me so busy for so long. I was really beginning to FEEL.

I had also developed a few physical manifestations of my grief. For one, my hair had started to fall out. Handfuls were coming out in the shower each morning. This was horrifying, as my hair was the one feature that I had always taken pride in. A not-so-healthy 20 pounds had found its way to me, the product of lots of comfort food and red wine. I had developed 2 bleeding ulcers. I needed iron infusions by intravenous. I needed a scope of my kidneys done. I was dehydrated. I had muscle pain. I had trouble sleeping. I was told I had complicated PTSD. Does any of this sound familiar to you? I posted this question to the grieving mothers in the Facebook group and was once again overwhelmed by their responses. Many also added lists of medications that were prescribed by their doctors and the inevitable side effects that they caused. Some had been diagnosed with heart conditions that they never had before. I had no idea that grief could cause so much trouble!

So, I began the lengthy process of self-care. Slowly, of course, because let's face it, I really did not care that much about myself at that time. I only cared that my son was gone. The first 2 years went by in a blur of brain fog while working long hours. Only when grief was focused upon, even researched, did I begin to understand what was happening to me, as well as to find ways to begin to reverse the effects of it.

There were some things that I knew helped me. The process of journalling, writing down memories as soon as they came to me for fear of forgetting them again. Sometimes, entire poems would come to me in the span of a few minutes, and it got to the point where I would keep the notepad and pen on my bedside table and write things down in the middle of the night. Why not, as I was not sleeping a lot of the time anyway. Here is an example:

Hold On

Early in the daylight hour

A songbird calls to me

High above the lighthouse tower

Way across the sea

A moment of enlightenment

Dawns just like the sun

And moves me to a purpose

Where before it there was none

Memories like shards of glass

Cut through the waves of time

Sharpened are their edges

By the daily grind

They fall away in steady rhythm

Though I grasp I can't hold on

They soften and then melt away

Eventually they are gone

Ceasing to exist is only

To begin another way

Giving one more reason

To begin another day

On and on the years slip by

As they are known to do

They take my hand and lead me

One step closer to you

    There would be dozens more where that one came from. They will end up in a book of their own one day. My point is this: when you are moved to write, I urge you to take the opportunity to get it down on paper, or onto your computer. It could be gone by morning. Morning could bring a grief day and once again, you will not feel like or be able to string many cohesive sentences together. It does not have to come out in poetry either. Sometimes just writing the exact words that you are feeling is beneficial, no matter if it happens to be a string of profanity colorful enough to give an entire boatload of sailors a little color in their cheeks! What you are going through is profound.

Grieving the loss of your loved one is profound. Honor it.

I also found that the more research that I did about death, the process of dying, near death experiences, life after death, energy, spirit, sound frequencies, meditation, mindfulness, and manifestation, the more that my fundamental belief system had begun to change. Some of the things that I feel are undeniable are these: we are energy, and energy cannot be created or destroyed. We just are. The body is simply a vessel that we use to get around in while we are here. It was easy for me to see that once Colton left his body behind, this vessel that was diseased and that no longer served him, that my son was no longer in there. Yet, over time, the thought that his energy still exists, has been a source of comfort to me. I have recently heard of this analogy, and it rings true for me: universal consciousness is like the ocean. If I scoop a cup of water from the ocean, that would be the spirit, (still part of the greater consciousness), now dye the water in the cup a distinct color (I like purple, but you do you). The spirit is now personalized, individual, the soul. The cup is the body that the soul uses while it is here. It is all a part of the same thing. You are not the body. You are not the purple coloring. We are all part of universal consciousness. We are one. I watched a speech by a famous environmentalist that stated that the atmosphere that sustains us and planet earth contains all the breaths of all the inhabitants that ever were, from the dinosaurs to celebrities to your relatives past and present. What a way to show that indeed there is no real separation between us! I remember thinking that Colton and I shared the same air eventually, and even this small comforting thought brought me a measure of peace.

It is possible to control your thoughts, and if you do, chances are that you will have a better day than if you do not. Now, this is not easy. It takes training, dedication, and practice. I am no expert at this, but I sure want to be! Where your focus goes, energy flows. Thoughts become things. Randy and I focused on our move to where we wanted to be. I am a true believer that you can manifest what you want. However, it is not easy to only focus on the good stuff. Thankfully, there is more good than bad. Even after a tremendous, heart-shattering loss.

Gratitude changes everything. That may sound hokey to you but believe me, since I have begun to start my day with a list of thankyous for the things that I have, it has made a world of difference in how my grief feels. It has made a difference in how I feel physically as well. I am thankful every day. I am thankful for where I live, who I live with, who I call friends, those who love me (both here and across the veil.)

I only know what I have learned to be true through my own extensive research and can only bear witness to my own experiences. Eventually in your life, you must let go of those things that are no longer true for you and when you do, you begin to walk the path of peace. There is no more wondering. You just know what you know is true.

It is true that losing Colton has taught me so much. About him. About myself. About life and death. It is a natural progression that through my personal growth and healing, it becomes important to want to share what I have learned to try and help others.

So, since I had this time to try and process my grief and journal about my experiences, the thought occurred to me to start a grief blog. There was only one tiny problem: I had no idea how to build a website! Thus began my tumultuous relationship with YouTube...

Chapter 21

The Blog

My poor brain! I was no techie to begin with. Coupled with grief, I was really asking for it when I set about learning whatever I could to get started building my website.

First, I began navigating my way through countless, and I do mean countless YouTube videos on website building for beginners. I would find the ones that showed step by step instructions and I followed along in real time. Inevitably, I would run into a problem that I could not solve, and it would often frustrate me for days. Sometimes, Randy would get home from work and see real progress, and other times, all he would see is his wife, stuck scrolling through videos looking for the elusive bit of information that I needed to get to the next step. Once I was set up, I needed a theme. I needed some plugins to do different tasks, such as backing up all my hard work. I needed security. I needed to be able to add new posts every day. I needed to be able to add pictures, a way to subscribe, a newsletter....it was overwhelming to say the least! But I was like a dog with a bone, it just fascinated me. It engaged my brain to focus on something that let me learn some new skills, while still letting my grief be the main theme. I felt like I had a goal. I felt like I was doing something positive with my grief, rather than just sitting and wallowing in it. One thing that also kept me motivated was how proud Randy was of my efforts! His encouragement kept me inspired and confident that I was doing something worthwhile. Still, there were lots of grief days....

I was determined by this point to not get stuck in my grief. Colton would not want that for me. As it was, I often thought "what must he think of me? I look like I have aged 10 years!" I would look in the mirror and see the red puffy eyes, the broken blood vessels, the face that dissolves into tears so easily, the grey, thinning hair, the sheer exhaustion.

One of the only things that calms me is my view of the ocean. I have seen sunrises that have made me dissolve into tears, but they are tears of gratitude. There is a lighthouse, the Cape Mudge Lighthouse, directly across Discovery Passage on Quadra Island. It is a beautiful gift that I continue to receive, whenever I look out of my windows to the East. In front of that lighthouse is where most of Colton's ashes were scattered, so that we could 'keep an eye on each other.' Now, I know they are not there anymore. They could have made their way to Alaska or, depending on the tide, down the coast to Mexico. Or they were simply absorbed back into the environment. I am not sure why I could not let all the ashes fall from my hand that day. I just was not ready to let them all go. I know where the rest will go. I hope that will happen this year.

In the portion of my brain that belongs to a romantic poet, I often wonder if in some magical way, Colton orchestrated the move for us, chose the house with the view that I needed, moved all the puzzle pieces on our behalf until the last one clicked into place. And somehow along the way, www.griefinmocean.com was born.

I began to write. I had journalled off and on prior to this, but now, it all had somewhere to go. After I had written several posts, I made the decision to let friends and family know about it. I put the link on Facebook and shared my intention to be transparent about the struggles of dealing with the loss of a child, in hopes of helping other bereaved parents. I think most of the people I knew were shocked at first, I mean, who does that? Who bares their soul for anyone and everyone to see? Has she completely lost it? Believe me, some days I honestly thought I had. Overall, the feedback I received was that it was a positive, raw, fearless thing to do. I really did not care what anyone thought of me, but I did want them to truly understand what a grieving mother thinks and feels. Until it is your turn, until it happens to you, you just do not. How could you? I wish that no one had to understand grief of this magnitude. But it is better that they get a glimpse of what it does to a person through reading this than must lose their child to fully understand. I would not wish this level of pain on anyone. Anyway, I just did it for me, at least at the beginning. I needed to get it out. I needed to document my story, my thoughts, and actions. I needed to somehow keep Colton's memory alive.

In the mornings, while my coffeemaker was working its magic, I would stand at the kitchen sink, look out at the lighthouse, and have a conversation with Colton. Quite often, ok always, I would start to cry, and then suddenly I would feel cold across the top of my arms. Like someone stepped out of the fridge and gave me a side hug. Also, I would constantly see 11:11 or 3:33 or 5:55 on the stove clock, the microwave, the car radio, my cell phone...everywhere. I would stop and say, "hi honey" and sometimes I would feel cold on my upper arms. Was it all in my head? It does not matter. It was such a comfort and continues to make me smile whenever it happens. A year ago, I went to a Spirit Fair with my sister-in-law and got a reading done. It felt amazing when she told me "When you talk to him in the kitchen, he's standing beside you looking at the view."

Although I was feeling a bit stronger during the first 6 months or so, there were a few days that knocked me down flat. Here is a blog post from October 24, 2020:

Letter to Colton

I have been procrastinating all day. Yes, I know that you know that I got my chores done early, did the shopping, started the laundry, walked the dogs, everything that I knew had to get done. All done in silence and as if sleepwalking. Thankful that it is not an expectation that I be sociable as I carry out these tasks. Thankful that I am wearing a mask. One of fabric, one of grief. I know the front yard needs to be weeded, and the front entryway needs to be painted. Instead, I sit here frozen. My head hurts. I can feel my forehead crumpled as my eyes squint and my brows come together. The pain of losing you, the physical pain is now permanently etched into my face. I see it every day. It has aged me in a fiercely unfortunate way. Since I am alone, I find myself talking aloud to you, to God, the Source, the Universe, the Angels, to all and anyone listening, to ask to make sure that you are ok. And eventually I will be ok. And I cry. And I cry and tell you how much I miss you. And I let the pain roll down my face for anyone and no one to see. Time keeps marching onwards and here I am because nothing is changing except maybe that I am getting older and sicker, and you do not have to anymore. I have made it to my destination. I have made it to the island. It is so breathtakingly beautiful, and I am fully aware of every sacrifice it took to get here. So, I am making a conscious effort to make the very most of it. I am mindful every day as I look at the water that it is looking back at me and yes, it brings some comfort. Maybe in time, much more time, I can sit here and think of you and not cry so hard. Maybe my chest will not feel like it is caving in. Maybe I won't feel like I have been savagely beaten. Maybe I will have enough energy to get up and get on with my day. I look at your pictures and I cannot breathe. I would not wish this pain on anyone. It is crushing in its weight, and yet it is only I that must carry it around every day. As the wave of grief crests and passes over me, I am thankful all over again that not every day is this bad. Some days, I am thankful that this feels like one of the 'good' days...

Chapter 22

Learning to Live with Grief

Even now, I wonder how does one move forward? I have done the time, or so I thought. I have started on a path toward wellness. I walk more. I drink less. I cut sugar out of our diet. I even learned to bake without it. I am doing all the things. Even the 20 pounds that found me have left me again, and my hair is long and thick once more (still grey though!) And yet, I still wonder, can my heart really handle this in the long term? When does the suffering end? What will I do without Colton for THE REST OF MY LIFE?

When Barb and I went to see the psychic medium, she read both of us quite well. I recorded the session and listened to it several times. Colton even got to listen to it, as the first session happened while he was still here. I hesitated to play it, but only for a moment. In the first session, she said that I would outlive my son. I thought it might shock him, but then, he already knew he was terminal and there were a few things regarding his new wife that I thought he would be interested to hear. She had said that she would remarry and have children, which is something that she desperately wanted, and Colton could not give her. It gave him some peace knowing that she would be all right and end up happy. I remember watching as he listened to the recording. He was so serious, concentrating and occasionally nodding his head in agreement. I remember the psychic telling me that I would have trouble regarding my heart around the age of 60, but I would end up fine and indeed, I would live to be nearly 100! In the audio, you can hear me say f*#k, and she laughs. I had immediately thought, "Why would I want to live that long without my son?" But here is the thing; we do. I have already lived for 6 years since my son died. It is unfathomable, yet here I am. I know that the saying goes "life is short." But, if you have survived the loss of your child, life seems exceptionally long indeed! What am I supposed to do with myself now? With that fact comes a great deal of emotion that we do not come prepared for. There is guilt, helplessness, depression, anxiety to name a few. The rug of hope has been pulled right out from under you.

The guilt. I would put this emotion right up there with the other stages of grief. No mother is perfect, but we all want what is best for our children and try to make that happen. Each time Colton got sick, I felt terrible, like, "how could I let this happen? I am his mother, and I should be able to protect him."

When I was 26 and got pregnant with Colton, I was dealing with a list of health issues at that time. I had ulcers and issues with absorbing nutrients. My morning sickness was outrageous. I was constantly worried that I was a terrible host for this human that was doing his best to come out perfect. Somehow, I managed to gain a total of 20 pounds and Colton was born on his due date. The cord was wrapped around his neck, and he was an emergency cesarean birth. He was beautiful, 6 pounds and 8 ounces of perfection. Somehow, I even felt guilt around his birth. I had to be sedated at the last second, as my epidural had worn off, so I missed seeing and holding him first. The milk that I was able to produce for him was weak, a near-blue transparent color that I was terrified lacked what he needed for proper growth. With every cold, every infection, every surgery, then finally cancer, I carried so much guilt that it started to destroy me from the inside out, both physically and mentally. I know that my guilt is a lot to unpack, I just got so used to carrying it with me, you know?

The helplessness. This is the truth: It took me a long time to get my level of confidence back. I felt that since I lost Colton that I was a failure at motherhood. If I was a failure at motherhood, then it made sense (to me, anyways) that I was a failure as a wife, homemaker, employee, sister, artist, you name it. I could not handle things that I used to handle with ease. I was scared. I could not function.

The depression. Of course I was depressed. The days seemed endless. The sadness so complete that I was sure that I would never smile again. My chest felt so heavy, and every breath was labored. I would sit in the same spot for what was sometimes hours at a time, without the energy or reason to move. Yes, my mind and body were tired, and the rest was what I needed. Eventually, there was enough energy to read or watch videos that soothed my soul.

The anxiety. At times, I was totally immobilized. I could not leave the house. On good days when I felt like I could, I would find myself out shopping somewhere and have a full-blown anxiety attack where I had chest pain, I felt like I could not breathe, I would break out in a sweat. I would run to the safety of my car and sit and cry until I felt better, or at least different. To be honest, I still struggle with anxiety from time to time. I am not as social as I once was. I am still working on that one, for sure. There are days when I think about my son and how much I miss him, and ALL those feelings rush over me like it was the first time.

Yes, meditation has helped me. Yes, diet and exercise help, and I know my dogs like a good walk. Yes, writing, poetry and art have helped tremendously. Someday soon, I am going to learn how to play the acoustic guitar that Randy gave me for one of my birthdays years ago. My point is this: grieving, if left unchecked, might devastate you. Your life, your health, your job, your relationships. The things that help you in your healing process are not new. They are tried and true. There is no mysterious cure. It is a ton of demanding work, and the kicker is, at least on some level, you must want to do the work. You will get there when you are ready. No one can get you there but you. No one can give you directions to your path of peace. This is your journey, and yours alone. The journey is a long one, and quite often, it sucks. It is important for you to take all the time you need. This is about you now, no one else.

Ask yourself, what is the condition of your heart? Heading into my 59th year, the psychic/medium was right, I had a couple of vasovagal episodes that did validate that reading. Am I fine? Yes. Apparently, I am here to stay.

But that is not what I mean. What I mean is, "Is your heart open?" Has your heart condition changed since your loss? Throughout my spiritual journey, (which is how I refer to all the research that I did after Colton passed,) I have noticed major changes in how I view life. My heart has been broken. And sometimes, I feel as if it has been broken 'open.' I have described this transformation as follows: Do you remember the scene in that Christmas movie where a Grinch's heart grows 3 times its' size? It looks like it was a tremendously painful process! But once it happens, his expression changes from well, Grinchy, to.... loving. He has a change of heart. In fact, he sees his dog, and instead of yelling at him, his expression changes, and he tells him he loves him.

Somewhere along this journey, I have changed. Or at least, I am in the process of changing. I am different now, and it is for the better. I find myself letting go more. Of not only things, but of ways of thinking that no longer serve me. I am following the winding path that leads to peace. Sometimes it feels like I am following smoke through the woods, but that is just the way it is, because grief gets in the way. For example:

It was almost exactly a year after our move. It was a gorgeous weekend here and Randy and I had the opportunity to be out on the ocean in our boat. We had the chance to stay overnight in an off-grid Airbnb, a three-bedroom home set up in a private bay. On the way out the water was a little rougher than usual, but Randy handled the boat with no problems, and we were enjoying ourselves. About halfway to our destination, we started talking about spreading Colton's ashes, as I had not been able to do this yet. Just as we began talking about it, we saw the spray of a whale, so Randy slowed the boat in time for us to see a Humpback come up out of the water and show us a fin or two. He remarked on the coincidence of this happening just as we were talking about Colton. It was a special, magical moment. Shortly after, we arrived at the cabin and settled in, while the dogs were having a fun time exploring outside. We had set up prawn traps about a 10-minute ride from the place, and we were excited to collect prawns the following morning. I sunbathed on the deck while Randy took a kayak to the other side of the bay to collect a bucket of oysters that we cooked on the BBQ later that evening. The sky was blue, and the ocean was as gorgeous as ever.

We were up at 6 the following morning to run out and collect our prawns. Everything went perfectly and after returning to the cabin, 71 prawns were processed and bagged up and ready to take home. On the way home, the ocean was calmer than the day before, and we spoke about how wonderful it was to have the opportunity to do this, to live here, to have a boat and be out on the ocean exploring this beautiful place.

Then, as I was looking out at the sun reflecting on the water, it happened. A grief sabotage. Out of the clear blue sky, in the happiest of moments, after a wonderful weekend, came a picture in my head that made me close my eyes and feel the all-to-familiar stab of pain to the heart. This time the image was of my daughter in law and I washing Colton's body and changing him into his favorite outfit shortly after his passing. When this happened in 2018, I was in shock and did not remember much, but now, undistracted, the memory was brutally crystal clear. Graphic.

So, I sat there quietly dealing with this and eventually Randy looked over to see the tears rolling down my face and he asked me what was up. As I explained what had just happened to me, we both gained another level of understanding about how grief works. Sometimes, like just then, it swoops in with a gut-punch of a memory that nearly knocks you from your chair. And as swiftly as it comes, it goes, leaving you reeling with the impact. Fortunately, I was able to acknowledge the memory, validate it, send my love to Colton, and let it go. I am not always able to do that, so, for that I was grateful. After that, the weekend continued to be as lovely as it began.

This is not the first time that I have been grief sabotaged, and I can guarantee it will not be the last. I do not always recover that quickly. My mind is full of these images and memories of the trauma that I experienced while losing Colton. The pain that I feel when they flood my mind is as sharp as it was in the moment. Even more so, as I was numb with shock and disbelief when it happened. They remind me of so many things. Not only of the tragedy of Colton's illness and passing, or the feelings of helplessness and emptiness, but of the never-ending love that a mother has for her son.

On another beautiful blue day on the ocean, Randy and I had an interesting experience that I will never forget. We had been out all day on the water, and we were now making our way home. I noticed something landed on the canvas just above the front window of the boat. It was a huge dragonfly! I showed Randy, and then I tapped on the inside of the canvas, but it would not leave. I told Randy he wanted to come in, and I unzipped the canvas a few inches and sure enough, it came inside. We talked about how weird it was that this dragonfly was out over the ocean. Since he was not going anywhere, I became convinced that we were having a visit from Colton. Maybe not. But what if it was? I reached up with my fingers out and it jumped right on! So, that is how it rode all the way home to the wharf. Once there, I walked him out to the swim grid, and we just looked at each other for a minute. I thanked him for coming to visit us today. Then it flew off into the sunshine. It could have been just a blue dragonfly. It could have been a message that we were being watched over that day. It could have been a sign that Colton's soul was free. Of course, I had read the books about how when a loved one passes, they often send a dragonfly, butterflies, or ladybugs to visit those who are grieving to let them know they are ok. I can never be sure, but I also cannot count it out either. Hmmm.

As the years come and go, time starts speeding up. I am sure that other bereaved families feel the same, that it becomes increasingly difficult to maintain relationships that are connected to our child's passing. It makes sense. In our minds, and in all our pictures, our child remains the age they died. Colton's friends are in their 30s now, and their lives are busier than ever. They have families of their own. In fact, almost all of Colton's friends are parents. They are building careers, buying their first house, doing all the normal things that Colton should be doing. As I watch their children grow, it puts the passage of time into perspective. It shows me once again what I am missing as I will never be a grandmother. It forces me to realize that whether I am aware of it daily or not, I am moving forward with my life. I am trying to bring Colton along with me. There is huge comfort in that if I let there be.

I can only assume that this same explanation applies to some of my adult relationships that have disintegrated since Colton's passing. It just does not apply to them any longer, they do not think about it, and as the years continue to put space between us, the event that stays in my mind and affects my daily wellbeing has completely vanished from theirs. This is the truth. It is difficult for me, but I do understand it. Fortunately, I have also reconnected with friends that truly understand loss and who have been supportive of my grief journey. I now make a conscious, thoughtful choice about who I connect to, as it seems that my tolerance for anything negative in my life has seriously diminished.

Social media plays a role in this regard. I can post something about Colton, a milestone, or even something positive that is going on here on the island. It is easy to see who cares enough to reach out, comment, or even further, text me or give me a call. There are a few who have a son Colton's' age, and of course, I wish it were my son that was alive and out for dinner with me, or home for Christmas, or whatever. I would be lying if I said it did not affect me. What I am saying is this: it should not stop you from reaching out to a friend who has lost her only son. Oh, but you do not want to hurt me or remind me of my grief, is that it? Seriously? Do you think that for one second, I had forgotten? Just do it. Because if you continue not to, it simply moves you further and further down my list of friends that I know are true. For the love of all that is righteous, stop shutting out those who already feel alone. If it makes you feel uncomfortable to reach out, then perhaps you should take a moment and try to comprehend what life would be like if it were you suffering this loss. Then suck it up and pick up the damn phone. Has this happened to me? Yes. Does it make me unreasonably angry? Yes, yes it does. And sad, sad too.

Also, realize this: a grieving mother does not just miss her child at the age they were when they passed. We miss every chapter of their lives. Remember, we have a LOT of time to think. We review everything right from day 1. In my mind, I have re-lived everything that I can stretch my brain to remember about Colton. I remember a beautiful baby boy with a full head of dark hair, blue eyes, and a dimpled chin. The kind of baby that strangers come up to and say wonderful things to. I remember a resilient young boy who made friends easily and kept them forever. I remember a pre-teen trying to find his own style. I remember a teenager with a close-knit circle of friends. I remember the day he got his first job, when he bought his first car and learned to drive it. I remember the first girlfriends and the first heartbreaks. I remember all the pain and suffering. I remember every chapter of his. I will labor tirelessly to keep these memories alive. I am his mother, and I am fiercely aware that it is up to me.

Oh Colton, I remember a time when I thought that being your mom was the hardest job there was. But you were here and in hindsight you made it easy. Now I know that being your mom without you here is simply the hardest job ever. So, so much harder.

A bereaved mother has a faraway look in her eyes. I know that sometimes I have it. I have seen it in others. It is a space we have found that is in-between. It is a place somewhere after the death of our child, yet not in the present moment. It is rarely in the future. It is often in the past. It is a very confusing place to be. If only it was easier to control my mind. My thoughts and memories surrounding my loss had me stuck on the hamster wheel of my creation. Not by choice, but as a part of human nature. For a long time, I let the hamster wheel turn. Hell, I even oiled the thing, so it did not make that rusty metal squeaky sound. However, it does not take you anywhere except around in circles. It seems the options are as follows: You let your grief consume you. I mean, let's be real. It will consume you at first. Then as time passes, you may notice that you are a functioning shadow of who you used to be. You regularly get out of bed and take a shower. This is sometimes referred to as a good day. More time passes, and you discover for a fact that time does not heal all wounds. You feel cheated by this, but you realize that you will never "get over" this, so you will have to carry it. You must muscle up because it is heavy! It is going to take incredible effort on your part. There is nothing easy about being "here." But you do not have to be "there" all the time either. Give yourself the love that you once gave to your child. Stick a fork in that hamster wheel from time to time and give yourself a break. You need it. Sit in the now and really think about what is next for you. What did you love to do that you have forgotten for too long? Today is Day 1. Tomorrow is Day 1. You must make it what you need it to be.

One morning Randy and I were reading the paper, and an obituary caught my eye. It started with the words "My Journey Is Over." This woman named Lillian had written her own obituary! What a courageous and beautiful soul to take such an excellent opportunity to have the last word. She expressed the fact that, due to her terminal illness, she had the unique 'gift' to personally thank her team of family, friends, doctors, and nurses who had done so much for her. This got me thinking that I should write my own and update it often. I also thought back to the one that I wrote for Colton, and how much better of a job I could have done if he and I had written it together. I should have asked him. It would have been more Colton-y. There is a lesson here. My God, I have learned so many lessons over the last 6 years! I took a lesson from this woman who took a moment to comment on her time here. They were her words. In the end, time feels short, and we need to make it count, learn the lessons, become better people, to show love. (Spoiler alert, it is all that truly matters while you are here, and it is all you can take with you when you go. I watched.)

Sometimes when I am under a wave of grief, I end up with a grief hangover. Yes, this is a thing. I know that my grief will walk with me for the rest of my days. Remember the little black dust-ball that follows me? I am still learning how to help myself when it strikes. Whenever I am alone for an extended period, I know that grief will challenge me. Normally, I have Randy to talk to, or hold me when it gets bad. Sometimes, like when he goes on a hunting trip, it is all me. I usually start by making myself a to-do list that is impossible to achieve, to keep me busy. This is a mistake.

There is a lot of time to think. Colton is in the middle of my thoughts. The loss of my son is a gaping hole in the middle of everything. I can look back on the other side of the hole and see things how they used to be. All the good times and all the challenges and all the love that I would never ever change. At that time, I could see the hole coming, and there was nothing I could do to stop it. Now, all these years later, I am just trying not to fall in the hole. Imagine my back against a wall of Colton and all my memories, trying to inch my way along the edge of the hole, desperately trying to get to whatever the other side is without falling in. Sometimes, all I want is to fall in the hole. My point is this; too much time spent dwelling on what you no longer have is gut-wrenching and hard on the heart. It can lead to being swept up in a grief tsunami of your own making.

Now let me explain what I mean about the 'hangover.' It starts with being unable to sleep well when we are consumed with grief. I would wake up with a bad headache like I had gone on a huge bender. There would be extreme brain fog. So, I would get up and make coffee. Follow routine. Make the bed, feed the dogs, take a shower. Instead of doing these things in rapid succession, each task took an eternity. I would walk into the living room and pick up the dog toys. I would look at the ocean. I would not remember why I went there. I would go outside, certain that yard work was on my list. I could not stay on the task. I felt exhausted, disoriented. I would go inside and lay down, then get up, repeat. I would tell myself that those dogs are not going to walk themselves, then wander, still in a fog, around the neighborhood and let them sniff every little thing that they want to because I did not care how long it took.

The next day I would still be foggy and tired and end up disappointed in myself. I would vow to be productive. I drank a bunch of water. I walked the dogs on a different route down by the water. I mowed the lawns. Whoops....too much. I had wanted to get some shopping done but would end up too exhausted. But I would begin to feel better. I would watch a couple of uplifting videos on YouTube and call it a night. I finally slept. When I could wake up rested and clear-headed, then I knew that this grief hangover had passed. Whew! I made it through another one by myself. I spent these days alone for 2 reasons: 1, it is not my style to burden anyone with my grief, and there was always the possibility that Randy was out of cell range on a mountain somewhere. And 2, I most definitely know that this is my journey and, only I can navigate the 'hole' of loss and it is I that must learn how to care for myself when I occasionally fall in. Most bereaved mothers suffer and struggle in silence. They are in private online groups for a reason. Even though they may have support, this is a solitary path.

If you are in the 'hole,' and you expect a 'hangover,' my only advice would be to be kind to yourself. Please do not try to check off items on a list of things to be done. Listen to your body. Grieving is a physical as well as a mental activity, and it takes a tremendous toll on you. If you have that thick, cloudy feeling and your body is in pain, lay down and rest. Drink water to replenish all those tears because you know there will be more that needs to be shed. Listen to your breathing and try to be in the moment. Sometimes the moment sucks. However, the moment has value, immense value. That is grief. That is love.

Sometimes, it can feel like you are living the same day repeatedly. It is so hard to make a positive change when we are consumed by our grief. Is there any possible thing that we can do to change what happened to us? No. Every day we wake up and the outcome is the same. It can be easy to lose hope when you know that you will never see your child's face again.

There is a saying that speaks to the fact that if you continue to do the same things, you will never get a different result. That makes sense, right?

We have a choice to make. We can continue to feel trapped by our loss, or we can let it be a catalyst for change. If this sounds like pressure, then, disregard it. You will make the choices that are right for you when you are damned good and ready, and not before. There is no judgement here. I know that every day is different, even now.

I began to ask the questions: "What small change can I make today to improve my life now?" (keep a routine, take a walk outside, call or text a friend) "What lessons can I learn from this experience?" (life is short, time is precious, love is what matters) "Am I living in a way that would make my child proud of me?" (self-care, follow your passion, set goals).

Of course, there is no single answer that fits everyone. There never is. Everyone will grieve differently and in their own time. Some days, the good ones, the fog lifts, and we see a little further ahead of us. The journey of the bereaved parent is unwanted, unenvied, and uncharted. The only one who can decide where it will lead is you. Please do not give up. Tomorrow can be different.

You will be faced with difficult days. There are days that are only special to you. They are milestones.

They hurt. This blog post tells the story about Colton's milestone birthday:

As if I could forget your birthday. Or that look on your face on Christmas morning. The words you would put onto a Mother's Day card. The way you would smile and pat your belly like an old man after one of my roast beef and loaded mashed potato dinners. I remember everything. It is a blessing and a curse. I remember shaving your head, while your hair was so thick that it took three or more tries to get it looking the way you liked it, all the while talking for hours. I remember what you like to wear, nothing fancy, as long as it was black. I remember all your fashion stages as you were growing up, from the blonde tips to the chains around your neck, and all those track pants, hoodies, and hats. I remember measuring your foot against my thumb as I held you after you were born, and I remember how you like them hanging out of the blankets on your hospital bed so I could grab them as I walked by. I remember how your toes always cracked as you walked across the floor. I remember your face so clearly, your beautiful blue eyes and dimpled chin, and a smile that could melt my heart. I remember you. I remember details until I can no longer breathe.

Milestones are like missiles aimed straight at the heart of a grieving parent. We cannot dodge them. It is as if we have huge targets on our backs. They are coming for us. All year I watched your friends turn

30. The celebrations, the cakes, and the candles. I watched their children grow. I watched as they got new jobs, new homes, new reasons for the new smiles in the recent photos. Today I posted old photos with old smiles because that is what I have left. Old memories. Still, I will never give them up as they are keeping you alive in my mind, and they are what keeps me moving forward, passing all these milestones. 30 years ago today, I became your mother. I only had you. You were all I needed. Some days I do not feel like a mother anymore, as I watch those I know love and care for their children and even some with grandchildren. It becomes even more difficult to identify with them. I am on the sidelines. I am the one wearing the sad smile. I am the one that wishes them a happy birthday and likes their photos on Facebook while I cry for you. I can feel a part of me shut down. Those feelings are not for me anymore because you are gone. I was cheated out of them, and now I am left with memories and milestones. They make me wonder. I wonder who you would be today. I wonder who you would love. I wonder if you would have children, how many, and who they would look like. I wonder what job you would have and if you would like it. I wonder if you would still pursue your music. I wonder how you would spend your days. I wonder what you would do for fun. I wonder how you would age, and how the wrinkles and grey hair would add character to your handsome face. I wonder if you would be happy. I wonder what we would talk about.

Then, I imagine that I already know all the answers. I have built such a wonderful and happy life for you here in my mind. We have endless conversations. You come with me when we are out on the ocean, at the cabin or at the beach, even when I am walking the dogs. You are with me. Because I remember you. To Eternity and Beyond, I remember you.

Yes. That is what milestones are like. So, so hard.

Chapter 23

Something New

As time passes, and you begin to do the work of healing, you will want to try something new. You may feel the need to reinvent yourself. I know that I began to wonder "Who am I now?" "Where do I go from here?" I had endured, I had survived everything. I had survived the thing that I had feared the most. When the time is right, and you can finally see through the fog, there is a certain freedom there. For me, I no longer feared death. I know that when it is my turn to go, that Colton will be there to help me. But until that time comes, I can focus on what I want to do for the rest of my days. I can follow my passion. I can do whatever puts me on my path toward peace. So, if you feel strong enough, say 'yes' to a new opportunity.

After a year I was contacted by the Head Office of the company I work for. The regional manager for the island had suggested my name and I am grateful that he did. The job required driving to Langley for a week of training, then taking home a laptop and monitor and working from home. I remember being so excited and more than a little freaked out about this. Was I ready? This job involved floor planning with tiny fixtures and precise placement of objects in complicated computer programs. It was completely different from anything else I had done so far in my career. Yes, I was ready. This job came to me at exactly the right time!

I found that working from home was sometimes more of a challenge than I had expected it to be. I had 2 dogs that wanted to be let in and out all day. It required more discipline than I had needed for the last year. I had to get up early now and be focused all day. I had a schedule now, that I had to do chores around, as everything else at home still needed to get done. I now had to learn how to do zoom calls...that was new! The work itself was detail oriented and frustrating at times, but I really enjoyed it. I had to kick my brain into high gear as there was so much to learn! I met new people and formed relationships based on the shared experience of working in similar roles in the stores here in B.C. as well as Alberta. My days went by so fast, and I started to feel like I was back in the land of the living. I did share my story with the people that I worked closely with and with my supervisor, and I am glad that I did. For this reason: I knew that eventually I would have a grief day. Actually, I had many grief days. Thankfully, most of these days were spent alone, and I was able to just focus on the tasks I was performing, and it did not matter if I was crying or not. There was more than one occasion, when I had to be on a zoom call with the team, that I had bad brain fog. It was so bad that I had difficulty navigating the different computer screens and tabs and had to ask them all to have patience as I was having a moment of difficulty. Yes, there were a couple of awkward silences. Yes, I am certain that there was a conversation or two after the end of the call. But, over time, I was able to complete the tasks as good or better than the rest of the team. I learned my job, and they all learned a bit about grief. There were many days where I struggled and thought there was no way that I was able to handle the stress of grief and the stress of the importance of the job I was entrusted with. There were many days where I was so thankful that I did not have to leave the house.

Winter on the island is so grey. There is so much rain. It is heavy. There are many weeks where, not only could I not see the ocean, but I could also not see across the street! I would hear the foghorn in the early morning. It is an eerie, mournful sound. I would smile because it felt like me, just trying to navigate through the fog. I would make my coffee and put on my slippers, wrap my blanket around me and go to work. It was perfect in so many ways. The project that I was working on lasted just over a year, and then it was time to box up the computer and monitor and ship it back to Head Office. I had a sense that this was the beginning of a new chapter once again.

As I had successfully completed that job, my regional manager had produced a plan to send me to help stores around the island as needed. This was to be the total opposite of what I had been doing, as I would be working freight, building displays, running a checkout, slicing, and packaging bread, whatever was needed. It was going to be boots on the ground, hard physical work like I had done years ago. This job was unique in the fact that I did not know anyone when I arrived in their store, and they had no idea who I was.

The first couple of days are awkward, like you would expect, but they fly by immersed in the job. You settle into the routine of the store and the hotel. You get to know the team. So, here is what happened in each store; by the end of my time in each location, I had formed relationships with the team members who found me approachable, and who needed to tell their stories. Once again, I was a grief magnet! It was as if I was wearing a sign that said "I know about grief. Let's talk. " Maybe 'grief magnet' is not the right name for this, but it aptly describes what was happening wherever I went. I found it to be so rewarding. Plus, after a 2-week stay in each store, I was able to honestly answer whatever questions the regional manager had for me, as he valued my opinion and knew my ability to connect with the team.

I was always eager to hear my reviews as well. What did the team think of me? Apart from being thankful for my long hours of help and creativity, I provided the 'mom energy,' that many of the team members needed. The conclusion that I draw from this experience is this: Often, people just need someone to talk to. They need someone who has life experience, someone who has experienced great loss.

I would never have guessed that what I had been through would change me to the point where this would end up being me. But there is something bigger at play here. This all-encompassing grief, this life-altering experience that cracked open my heart, has left me quite different than I was before.

I wish that this version of me just spontaneously appeared one day, and nothing tragic had to happen to facilitate it. However, is that EVER the way life goes? Not for me, that much is certain. I had a great many lessons to learn along the way. I still do.

I have been given the opportunity to do a few special projects since that time. A few weeks here, a few weeks there, working extremely hard and connecting with people who need to tell their story. A young man that was Colton's age had recently lost his friend in a vehicle accident and was navigating his grief. His relationship with his mother was strained. He had just moved home to help after the loss of his father as well, who was a police officer. He had a lot to deal with! He poured his heart out as we worked together. He needed a mom to talk to. When I told him my story, and that my son was his age, he immediately got up and gave me a hug and said he was so sorry, that no mom should have to endure that. It was exactly what I needed at that moment. It has been stories like this that tell me that the purpose that I will serve for the rest of my days will involve simply listening. People around us are going through struggles and life events every day. That is why, now more than ever, we need to be there for each other. People want their stories to be heard. It makes us feel less alone.

I have met other bereaved parents. The way in which they lost their child varied, but the feelings are the same. Grief unites us.

This year, 2024, brings another season of change. Now that the 30th anniversary of my career has passed, I have retired from my current role and began another within the company. I know that Colton would be so proud of me and celebrate my milestones as well. I often think that he is cheering me on from across the veil between here and there. It is beliefs like those that keep me going, really. It is part of the ongoing narrative in my head. The one of how things are supposed to be. This brings me back to a previous question: What if this had all been planned out ahead of time? On the 2nd visit to the psychic/medium, the conversation was quite different. She spoke of a soul contract between Colton and me. This had apparently been agreed upon before either of us were born. It was that I would be his and he would be mine, that he would leave me quite early in my life and I would mourn him for the rest of my days and that I would grow from the experience. I looked at her in disbelief! I said "That is the crappiest contract I have ever heard! Who would sign such a thing?" She just smiled, and told me that we have a soul family, and we decide ahead of time what story will take place once we are here, based on what we personally need to work on. This enables us to learn a great many lessons, become better people, and improve humanity as a whole. Honestly, I took the reading for what it was and assumed that she was right, and that I had more lessons to learn, and a lot of personal growth to accomplish during my lifetime. But it also could have been a gigantic load of crap.

Now, of course, you can take that for what it is worth. Everyone believes in something different, and we all have freedom of choice. It took me years to accept this line of thinking, but eventually, with the fact that Colton died, and I am left to figure out the rest of my life and what it all means, I had to just go with it.

There are so many belief systems to choose from. Where do we go when we die? Are our loved ones able to contact us? There seems to be overwhelming evidence that this is possible. As easy as a text message, a piece of energy that can be sent in real time to someone on the other side of the earth. Does it not seem possible then, even probable, that we would be able to send a thought, energy, to someone without a text message? I believe so. In my mind, it is not that big of a stretch. But until the day when I finally figure out how to do that, I shall continue talking to myself, and him, and feeling like (as my dad might have said) I am one brick short of a load.

Still, I am more comfortable with this practice as time goes by. It just feels natural.

This year I started thinking about Goals and Perspective. Many see the new year as a reset, a fresh start. The grand beginning to achieving the new goals they have set for themselves. What is your goal?

For those who have endured great loss, perhaps it is simply to Go. On. After. Loss. There is so much work that needs to be done to achieve a level of self-care and mental health to simply survive the normal workday. For some it takes an extraordinary amount of effort to clean and maintain a home or plan and prepare meals when the thought of leaving the house seems overwhelming. But we humans... We are such a resilient bunch! We pick ourselves up. We see through the fog, and we carry on. We come to realize that we indeed are here to experience all this life must show us. To revel in the joys and wallow in the lows and find the lessons and learn from them and change, improve and grow. Today is a wonderful day to do just that. If you woke up today, you already have so much more than many of our loved ones did.

These days, I work extra hard to feel grateful every single day. I make the effort to say my Thank Yous(s) each morning. Some mornings are easy, like when I see a truly magnificent sunrise. Some take more effort, and I must dig deep, but I do it. I have made it my goal. Today is a day for goals. Every day is. Start here. This year will bring more change. There will be moments of happiness to build us up. There will be moments of pain and sorrow where we will need to show a great deal of resilience. So go ahead and make goals. Make Goals with Perspective. Go. On. And. Love. Go. On. And. Learn. Get. Out. And. Live.

Until then,

I don't know a lot about a great many things

But I do know a lot about grief

I hope that these words and the feelings they bring

Will give tired hearts some relief

A body in pain can move forward again

Emptied arms can still give a hug

A mind in much turmoil can find purpose within

And drag you right out of the mud

Weary bones still travel to places unknown

To find friends they have yet to meet

Crying eyes can still see the sunrise

And a broken heart still beats

The End

(There Is No End)

Photos

Colton and his proud momma (a Barb photo)

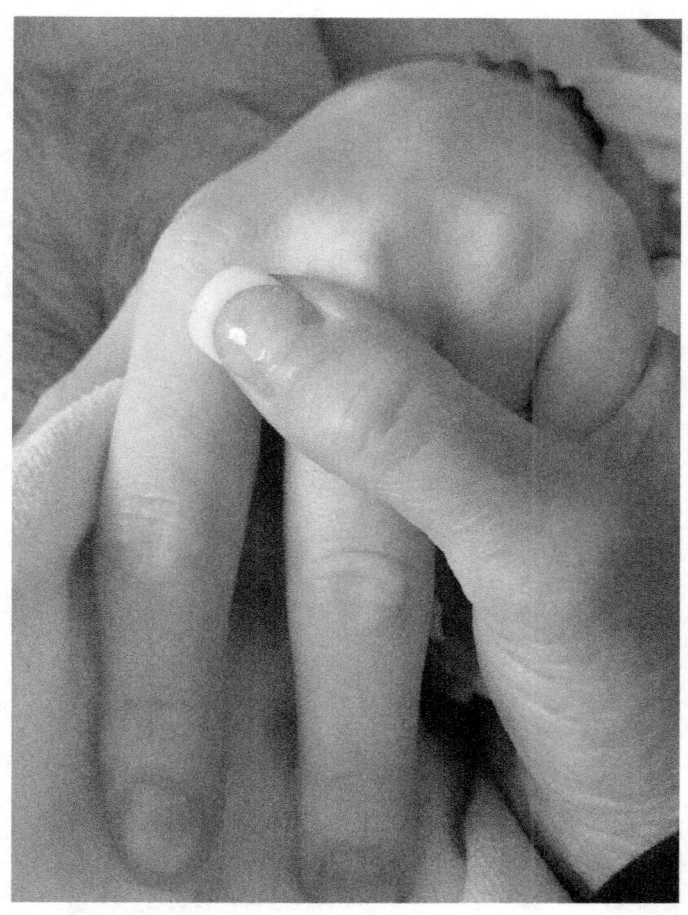
Hanging on for dear life

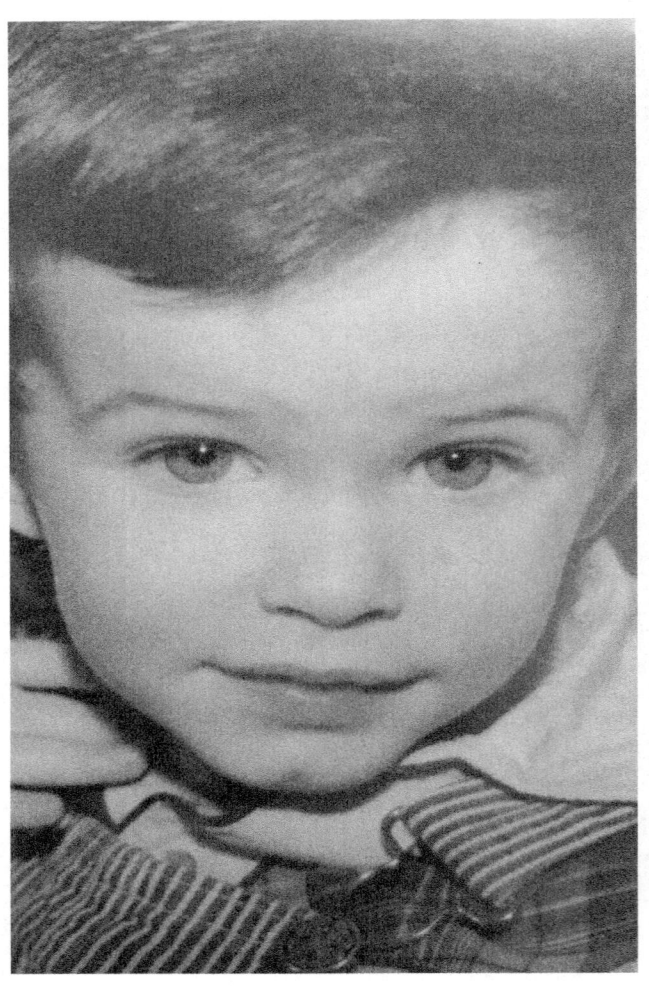

Perfection

Sometimes you simply must believe in the signs

The beautiful blue dragonfly ocean visit

A hug in Hospice House (a Barb photo)

Me and my beautiful friend Barb (a Dave photo)

Me and my Randy at the lake cabin

About the Author

Born and raised in the Okanagan Valley of B.C. Canada, Nancy has always felt at home near the water. She has a love of the arts, focusing on writing, poetry, and painting. This is Nancy's first book, but will not be her last, as she has found the process a cathartic and rewarding experience. Nancy and her husband Randy now live in Campbell River B.C. where she looks at the ocean, has kitchen chats with Colton, and continues to carry her grief as she journeys toward peace.

Acknowledgements

Randy, thank you for your never-ending love and support as I navigate my grief journey. Thank you for being my cornerstone. Thank you for looking after me when I could not look after myself. Thank you for riding out the storms with me. Thank you for showing me this beautiful place we call home. Thank you for being such a wonderful stepdad to Colton, both a positive role model and friend. Thank you, my love.

Barb, I cannot thank you enough for your friendship and loving support from the day we met until tomorrow. Thank you for letting me into your heart. Thank you for the love you showed Colton. He absolutely adored you. Thank you for giving me a safe place to land during the most difficult of times. Thank you for picking up the phone or answering texts at all hours of the day or night. You simply mean the world to me. Thank you, my friend forever.

Thank you to my brother Jim and my sister June Snow for being there to support me through this journey. You both showed up in so many ways with love and support for Colton as well as for Randy and me. Thank you both so much for taking care of Mom as she passed, knowing I could not be there. I have thought about this so often while drafting this book, as I understand what that looks like from ground zero. Your sister loves you both so much.

Sincerely, I want to say a huge thank you to the Prince George Hospice House and all the wonderful, dedicated, truly gifted people who work there. You made Colton comfortable. You made all his friends feel welcome. You provided much needed comfort for us all. For that, I am eternally grateful.

Michelle, meeting you was such a gift during that time. You were such a gift to Colton, and he loved you so. Please accept my heartfelt thanks for everything you did during Colton's fight and thank you for staying connected.

Colton, I know you know what I mean when I thank you for being the bright light in my life for the time you were here. Thank you for the light that you continue to shine so that I know which way to go. Being your mom was the greatest privilege of my life. What you endured in this life was unfair, and my heart ached as I watched helplessly while you took everything in stride. Thank you for teaching me how to die with dignity and grace. Thank you for giving me perspective. Thank you for making me a better person. Until the day when I am ready to go and I see your face again, keep dropping in for our kitchen chats, keep showing me those beautiful sunrises, keep thinking of me. Thank you for loving me the most, a mirror of my love for you.

Epilogue

That was a lot! I feel like a little sadness has lifted from my heart. I hope the same for you as well. My grief for Colton is always with me, but it has changed over the years. I still grieve for him every day. I do not expect that will change. But now, it is a little softer somehow, like the ocean waves wash the rocks on the beach until they are smooth and round. Some days the waves still crash and splash me in the face, but honestly, that is ok too. Everyone has a story to tell. The story is always one of love and grief, and it is a story worth sharing.

A Broken Heart Still Beats

By

Nancy Carswell

Printed in Dunstable, United Kingdom